INTERLINK
·HOME·ECONOMICS

Creative Textiles

Norma Heron and Sue Rainford

BLACKIE

INTERLINK
· HOME · ECONOMICS ·

© Norma Heron and Sue Rainford 1989
First published 1989

All Rights Reserved
No part of this publication may be reproduced,
stored in a retrieval system or transmitted
in any form or by any means electronic, mechanical,
photocopying or otherwise without prior permission of
Blackie & Son Ltd

Blackie & Son Ltd
Bishopbriggs, Glasgow G64 2NZ
7 Leicester Place, London WC2H 7BP

British Library Cataloguing in Publication Data
Heron, Norma
   Creative textiles.
   1. Textiles for schools
   I. Title II. Rainford, Sue III. Series
677
ISBN 0-216-92323-9

Printed in Great Britain by Scotprint Ltd, Musselburgh, Scotland

Introduction

Home Economics is a field of study which is concerned with all aspects of everyday living—the food we eat, the homes we live in, the people or family unit we live with or look after and the textiles we use in clothes and furnishings. All of these aspects are interrelated and that is why we have called this series *Interlink Home Economics*. The series is divided into four books so that we can concentrate on one main aspect in each book but, throughout, show its relationship to the other three aspects. The books are:

      Interlink Home Economics—Food
      Interlink Home Economics—Home and Family
      Interlink Home Economics—Child Development
      Interlink Home Economics—Creative Textiles

In *Interlink Home Economics: Creative Textiles* you will be looking at the way textiles, in many and varied forms, play an important part in our everyday lives. Originally, the name 'textiles' was given to any fabric produced by weaving. Today this definition has been broadened to include the whole range of products made from fibre—from rich velvets to parcel string.

Textiles are used extensively for clothing, by both young and old, by people from every culture and climate, and by people from every walk of life. They are also used throughout our homes—carpets, curtains, cushions and furniture covers being the most obvious uses. There are less obvious 'hidden' uses such as pipe lagging and insulation in electric cables.

Many manufacturing and service industries rely on textiles too. Think of the many uses in private and public transport, for instance.

Most of us have a favourite hobby, play a sport or enjoy a leisure activity. Textiles have a particular role to play for specialist clothing and the equipment required for such activities.

In hospitals and in other areas of medical care, textiles are an important factor—from surgical gowns to sticking plaster.

It will have been seen that we need a great variety of textiles because they are required for many different purposes. No one textile could perform all the tasks required of it, therefore the modern textile industry is constantly producing new products to meet the ever increasing demand that we, as consumers, place upon it.

If you look back through the previous paragraphs you can pick out seven common themes and these are the same as the ones identified by the GCSE National Criteria. They are so important that each time it is relevant we have indicated the theme in the margins of the book so look out for these catchwords: HUMAN DEVELOPMENT, HEALTH, SAFETY, EFFICIENCY, VALUES, AESTHETICS, ENVIRONMENT INTERACTION. We have added another—TECHNOLOGY. In addition look out for the DESIGN BRIEF symbol **D**. It is suggested that you keep all your design work and results of investigations in a folder. Add any interesting additional samples, pictures and magazine articles that are relevant so that your folder becomes a working 'log' of your progress.

As in any study, information is provided but the major emphasis is on investigations and using knowledge and skills to make decisions and evaluations on the basis of these investigations. The skills you will develop are those of investigation, measurement, communication and management, as well as manipulative and technological skills. The investigations which are so important that everyone should carry them out are called KEY INVESTIGATIONS ¶. There are others called INVESTIGATION EXTENSIONS ¶¶¶ which you can carry out if they interest you and you have time or you could always make up your own investigations depending on the problems you are trying to solve. In your discussions and answers you should be able to show how you have considered and related the common themes in evaluating your decisions and findings.

The purpose of this book is to stimulate interest in the study of textiles as a basic consumer commodity, putting particular emphasis on the creative aspects of wearing, choosing, using, making and decorating textiles. Throughout this book you may be surprised to learn how many different aspects there are to the design, making and use of textiles. Carrying out the investigations and design briefs will enable you to develop new skills and put previous knowledge and experience into context.

Without textiles, life as we know it could not go on. How many times have you used textiles today? Why do you think they have so many uses? Imagine a football match without textiles! No kit, no net, no corner flags, no banners, no crowd!

Acknowledgements

The authors and publishers are grateful to the following for permission to reproduce copyright material.

Dorma   page *12 (left)*
E. Gomme Ltd   page *12 (right)*
Courtaulds PLC   page *49*
C & A   pages *91, 127*
Biofotos   page *93*
Next   page *113*
The Hulton Picture Company   page *117*
Coats Viyella   page *133*
Jones and Brother   page *140*

Any photos not listed above were supplied by the authors.

Illustrations by Ian Foulis & Associates except for those on pages 19, 22, 26, 53 (lower), 74, 94, 97, 130 and 131 which are by Norma Heron.

Cover illustration by Evelyn Bautlett

Contents

1. Making Choices — 1
Let's Look at Textiles in Clothing — 2
Let's Look at Textiles in the Home — 11

2. Fibres, Yarns and Fabrics — 15
Let's Take a Close Look at Fabrics — 16
Let's Look at Fabric Structures — 25

3. Design Matters — 37
Let's Look at Design — 38
Colour — 46
Let's Experiment with Dyes — 55
Let's Look at Fabric Printing — 63
Let's Look at Texture — 71
Let's Look at Shape and Form — 77
Let's Look at the Use of Line in Design — 90
Let's Look at Pattern — 98

4 Consumer Awareness — 105

Let's Consider Textiles and the Consumer — 106
Let's Look at Shops and Shopping — 120

5 Technology in Clothing and Textiles — 129

Let's Look at Recent Changes in the Production of Textiles — 130
Let's Look at Technology and the Consumer — 136

Index — 142

1

Making Choices

MAKING CHOICES

LET'S LOOK AT TEXTILES IN CLOTHING

AESTHETICS

We all wear clothes and we all manage to look different! Clothing communicates to others what sort of person we are. When we meet someone for the first time, their clothes will tell us quite a bit about them before even getting into conversation and of course, our clothes will be telling them about us. Basically, what we can learn from other people's clothes includes the age group and obviously the sex of the person, sometimes their occupation (particularly if they are in uniform or in similar 'workwear'), and often the mood that they are in.

VALUES

Our clothes reflect our character, our social status, our occupation, our cultural background, often our religion and our general attitude to life. Contrast a bank clerk with a 'punk rocker', for instance. One conforms to an accepted standard and the other deliberately breaks away and attempts to shock and maybe even intimidate. Even with school uniform, it is fascinating to see how individual pupils will attempt to 'bend the rules' to look slightly different.

Our choice of clothing is very wide, shops and catalogues offering a great range, but we are also influenced by clothes we see on others, friends, in magazines and on TV. Fashion is for ever changing and designers generally aim their new ideas at the younger generation. Of course, it is not just the clothes themselves, but the whole 'look' that is created that is important—accessories, jewellery, hair style and make-up—these play their part too.

When we are very young, our parents choose and buy everything for us. At what age did you first choose some article of clothing for yourself? By their early teens most young people have a very real sense of what they want and how they wish to look. Of course, mistakes can easily be made and a fashion trend can look marvellous on one person but dreadful on another. As we mature, our taste in clothes change and often becomes more conservative, whereas the young are always prepared to experiment.

In the middle years people tend to know what suits them and are prepared to pay for fewer but better-quality clothes.

In old age many people are living on a limited income and have little money to spend on clothes. They are also less active and may be handicapped, they also feel the cold more and this has a big influence on their choice of clothing.

KEY INVESTIGATION

Choose three members of your family who each fit into one of the age groups listed below. Try to choose one from each group and include yourself.

- A 0–5, 6–10, 11–13
- B 17–20, 21–30, 31–40, 41–50
- C 51–60, 61–70, 70+

Collect information about the kind of clothes they wear.

Construct a table to show the age group and type of clothing each of the groups wears.

(There are many ways of constructing tables, they should be easy to read and suit your needs.) Here is one suggestion you may like to use.

Type of clothing	A	Self	B	C
e.g. Underwear Day wear—summer winter Outerwear Nightwear Footwear Leisure wear Jewellery Accessories etc.				

▷ ANALYSIS

1. Which age group possesses the most varied items of clothing?
2. Which age group possesses the least items of clothing?
3. Which age group spends most on clothing?
4. Which age group spends least on clothing?
5. Put the items of clothing into groups headed
   a for protection,
   b for modesty,
   c for status, etc.

▢ EVALUATION

1. Compare your own attitude towards buying clothing to that of an older member of your family.
2. What influences you most in the purchase of clothes and accessories?

Compare the type of clothes you wear today with that of a period in the immediate past.

What in general has influenced the changes?

Choosing clothes

AESTHETICS

As you will have noticed, identical clothes can look completely different on different people. Individuals grow at different rates and inherit certain characteristics. Some people are of normal weight,

MAKING CHOICES

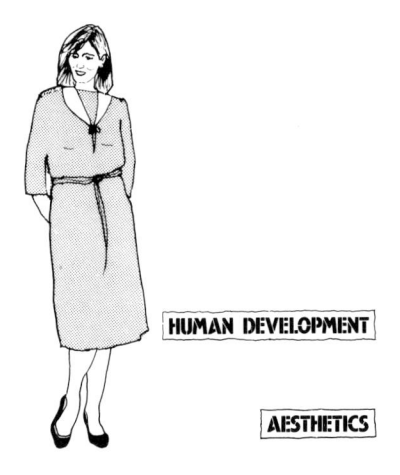

others over- or under-weight. Everyone moves and stands differently and has different natural colouring. As well as these factors there are other more practical considerations which affect choice, such as:

- cost,
- durability,
- availability,
- suitability for purpose.

It is important to understand the place of all these factors in the purchase of an item of clothing.

Firstly, let's look in detail at how body shape can affect the way our clothes look.

Height and weight together give an overall silhouette and if we can come to terms with our shape we can certainly learn to live with our often less than perfect figures. Bear in mind that there are times such as during pregnancy in women, when our shape may alter drastically.

Figure shapes can be put into broad categories. These are best described thus:

- square, straight body with little or no waist, can look 'dumpy' on short person. The 'sexless' shape of young children.
- a taller straight silhouette can look elegant.
- broad shoulders tapering to narrow hips, typical adult male silhouette.
- so called 'pear' shape in women, narrow shoulders, broad hips.
- the 'hour glass' figure, a balanced top and bottom with narrowing at the waist.

How best do you think clothes might be chosen to suit these differing figure types? Actually, there can be no hard and fast rules because every person is an individual who has freedom of choice. However, it is useful to have a few general guidelines.

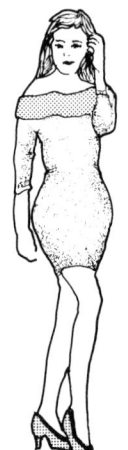

HUMAN DEVELOPMENT

AESTHETICS

4

CHOOSING CLOTHES

AESTHETICS

Colour: Dark colours are generally slimming to a broad figure, light colours tend to exaggerate size. By using dark and light separates, a top-heavy or bottom-heavy figure may be visually balanced.

Line: Vertical line in garment design is known to elongate and visually 'slim' a plump figure, horizontal line will add width to a very thin shape.

Pattern: Large, bold pattern can swamp a petite figure but can help visually to 'break up' a larger body size. In the same way small patterns can look lost on a large person. Using stripes, either broad or narrow, vertical or horizontal can have a dramatic effect.

Texture: Shiny surfaces catch and reflect the light therefore are inclined to make the figure look larger, matt textures are more slimming. In the same way, hairy fabrics add bulk but smoother fabrics do not.

It must be remembered that every fabric has its own characteristics. It can be dyed or patterned in a number of ways and then can be made up into any number of differently styled garments. When faced with the many problems that awareness of all these factors brings, it is easy to understand how confusion can arise and why so many people resort to impulse buying.

Designers and clothing manufacturers also have to face similar problems. Their role is to produce garments that will appeal to people of many different age ranges, figure types and budgets. An indication of how they do this is explained in Section 3. Manufacturers of ready-made clothing and makers of commercial paper patterns do all they can to help the consumer make satisfactory decisions.

Some shops specialise in garments for a particular age range, such as *Mothercare* or *Top Shop*, some cater for special sizes such as *Evans*, *High and Mighty* or *Long Tall Sally*.

Most stores such as *Marks & Spencer*, *C & A*, *Littlewoods* and *BHS* stock a range of clothing for all ages, sizes and budgets. The clothes are generally arranged in different sections to make selection easier. Sizing of garments is always a problem because some manufacturers cut their garments generously and some skimp. It is often a matter of trial and error to determine which make and range give you a good fit.

Sizes on paper patterns are standardised and these can be found in a table on the back of each pattern envelope.

KEY INVESTIGATION

Your teacher will provide you with a number of labelled fabric swatches. Examine each and enter your comments on a table similar to the one shown on the next page.

MAKING CHOICES

Swatch	Fibre	Weight	Colour	Texture	Structure	Pattern
A	50% Mohair 50% Wool	light/ medium	Royal blue	Open, fluffy	Knitted	None

▷ ANALYSIS

1 Take each fabric in turn, and suggest a suitable garment that could be made from it.
2 Imagine three different people of either sex with different figure types.
   Sketch an outfit for casual day wear for each person.

☐ EVALUATION

1 Why do you think an appreciation and knowledge of fabric types and garment styles is important?
2 How does this information help you in selecting garments for yourself?

INVESTIGATION EXTENSION

Try this investigation if your school has a uniform.
1 Within your year group at school there are many different figure types. The current uniform for girls is a skirt and blouse with either a V-necked jumper or cardigan and, for boys, shirt, trousers and V-necked jumper.

Work in groups to
a Identify the main figure types within the year group.
b Draw up a questionnaire to discover what the girls' and/or boys' views are on the present uniform. Try to question them on as many aspects as possible, e.g. styles, colour, material, availability, cost, etc.
c As a result of the above information and research, either design a completely new uniform or modify the present one. Keep in mind the cost, materials used, colour, ease of production and purchase.
d If possible compare the price of a complete uniform which can only be purchased from one supplier, with one where the various items of uniform can be bought from a number of different shops or from a chain store.

SHAPE IN GARMENTS

2 Your local keep-fit group are to give a demonstration of their skills at a Festival of Health and Beauty. Taking into account the various ages and figure types of the group, either design an outfit to be worn or collect together pictures of ready-made garments they could wear. Cost the outfits as accurately as possible.

Evolution of shape in garments

AESTHETICS

TECHNOLOGY

If you have cut out a garment using a paper pattern, you will have noticed the many and varied shapes that go together to make it up. These shapes are produced with the aid of 'basic blocks' which are derived from standard sets of body measurement (see below).

> Basic blocks are produced for various parts of garments. Usually, these are bodice back and front, skirt/trouser back and front and sleeve. The blocks are made from stiff card and the designer uses them as the basis for a wide variety of different styles by adapting them from simple shapes to more elaborate ones.

When using such shapes, you will have noticed that there is a considerable amount of waste fabric left after cutting out. This waste is costly and in commercial terms is cut down to a minimum by using highly sophisticated equipment including computers.

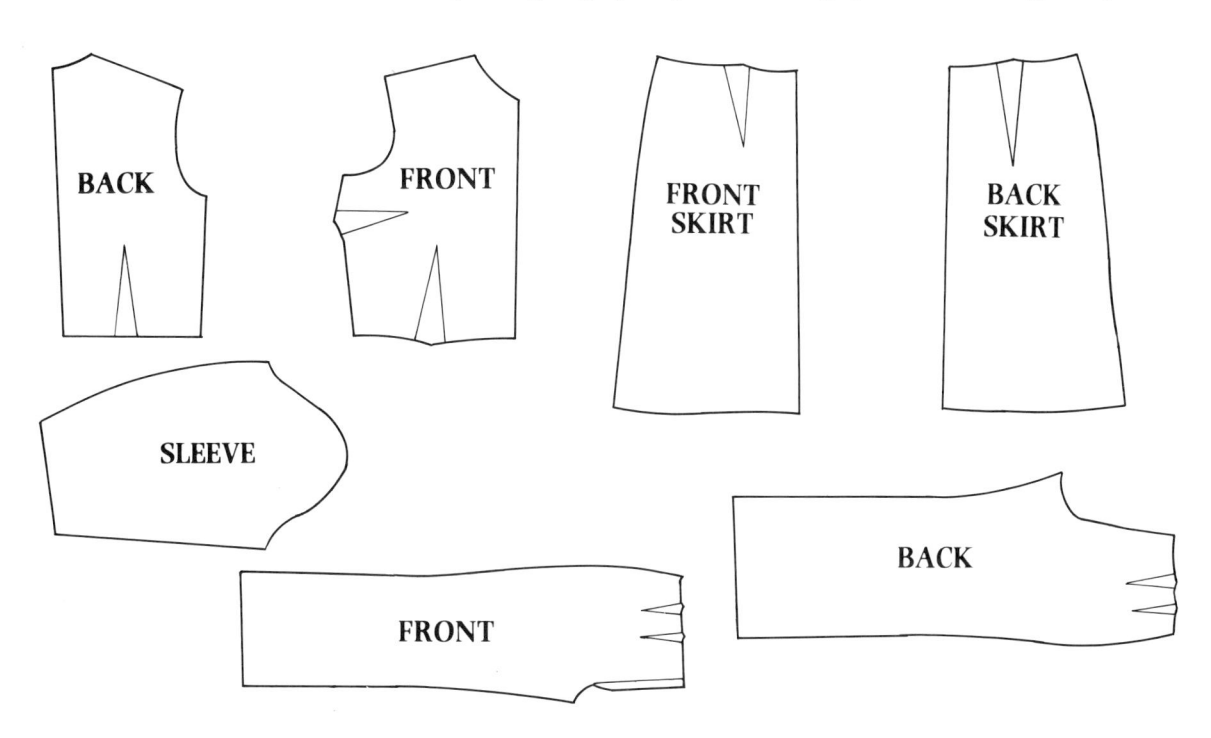

MAKING CHOICES

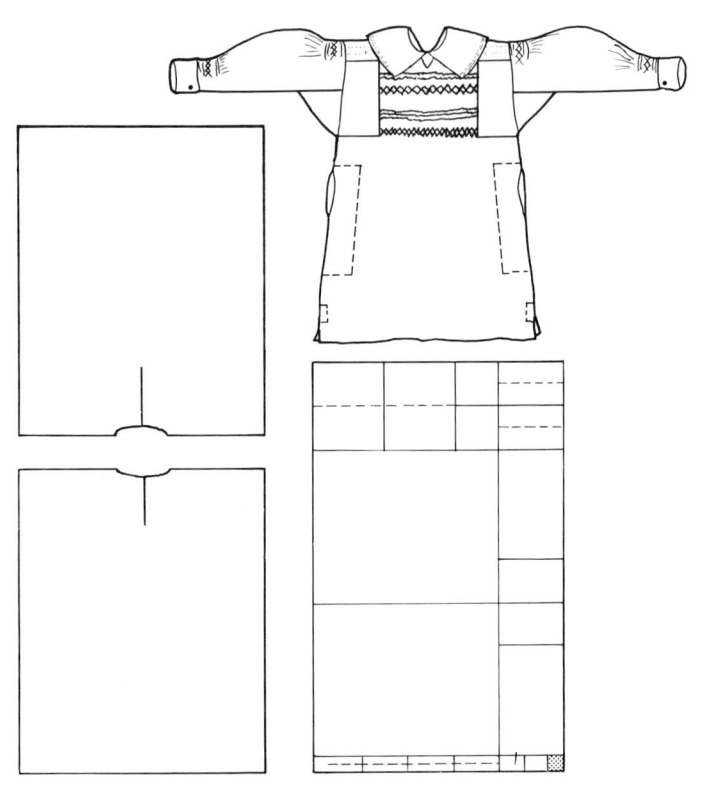

Originally, there would have been no waste because garments were made from actual lengths of fabric woven in certain widths depending on loom type. For example, English working smocks of the 19th century were made from a series of rectangles which were put together to form a very basic garment. There was no right or wrong way as both back and front were identical. Some smocks were embroidered to show the type of occupation of the wearer, e.g. woodcutter, shepherd, wheelwright.

Earlier draped garments like the ancient Greek chiton were made by simply wrapping the fabric length around the body and securing

SHAPE IN GARMENTS

ENVIRONMENT INTERACTION

it with a girdle and pins. Other garments made in different parts of the world depended on climate and natural sources of raw materials. The South American poncho and the Indian sari are examples of garments made from lengths of fabric with little or no sewing.

VALUES

> An old proverb in John Heywood's *Proverbs of the English Tongue* 1546, states 'I shall cut my cote after my cloth'. At the time there was a law in force which allowed no more than three yards of fabric to be used for a long gown. Today, 'cutting your coat according to your cloth' is still used as an expression meaning 'live within your means'.

EFFICIENCY

Ingenious uses of narrow lengths of fabric developed during the Middle Ages when simple cutting of the fabric into rectangles enabled people to make clothes which fitted their bodies more comfortably.

Wealthy people continued to wear full, long and heavily gathered clothes which gave them a stately appearance and proved that they did not have to do any manual work.

Slight variations in cutting to produce more shapely garments came about over a period of some hundred years. For instance, a simple shirt or shift is still being worn as the favourite T-shirt of today.

AESTHETICS

The highly-fitted clothing worn by the men and women of the 17th century to the 19th century culminated in the elaborate costume of the Victorian era. In those days, clothes were made mainly by local dressmakers and tailors but with the beginning of the paper pattern industry in the 1860s 'home' dressmaking became popular.

Today we can choose from a wide range of styles from a number of major paper pattern makers.

MAKING CHOICES

Journals, magazines and newspapers keep us up to date with the styles available and often offer patterns by mail order or include selected ones free with the magazine.

The process of designing and producing patterns involves many different skills. The flow chart below shows how this is done.

DESIGN DEPARTMENT	Ideas gathered, drawings submitted, altered and modified before they are approved. From hundreds 40 to 50 will be selected for production.
DRAPING DEPARTMENT	Sketches are created in muslin to follow 'line' and 'look' of sketched garment. Muslins then taken apart to make master pattern in heavy paper.
TESTING ROOM	Pattern made up in fabric. Checked for detail, comfort, wear and design. Then checked against illustration to ensure it is correct in every detail.
PRIMER DEPARTMENT	The primer sheet of instructions and diagrams of garment worked out. Information for the back of the pattern envelope laid out.
ART DEPARTMENT	Illustrations for front of pattern envelope. Every detail must be correct, even to number of buttons.
GRADING DEPARTMENT	Grader computes the variations and draws the graduations for the various sizes. Each size is transferred and cut to be sent to the printing plant.
MEASURING DEPARTMENT	Quantities of material required for garments. Pattern pieces laid out in most economical way for each size.
LAYOUT DEPARTMENT	Polaroid takes layout to be printed on primer sheet.
FABRIC OFFICE	Vast collections of sample fabric are collected to be used when illustrating and designing.
PATTERN PRODUCTION	Master pattern printed on to tissue paper to go into pattern envelopes.
COLOUR WORK DEPARTMENT	Art work for envelopes, counter catalogues and other publications are printed.

KEY INVESTIGATION

Make a list of articles of clothing and accessories which are worn today by people of your own and different cultural backgrounds which make use of lengths of fabric with little or no cutting and sewing.

SHAPE IN GARMENTS

▷ **ANALYSIS**

Tabulate your results as shown.

Garment	Country of origin	Sex	Colour	Type of fabric	Decoration
Sari	India	F	Bright or pastel	Silk or muslin or polyester	Border patterns, embroidery or printing

☐ **EVALUATION**

ENVIRONMENT INTERACTION

What reasons can you give for these garments being worn?
How does culture, climate or gender influence your choice of clothing generally?

INVESTIGATION EXTENSION

Using only squares and/or rectangles, design a casual top to cover swimwear when going to or from the beach. The only shaping which can be given to the garment is by gathering or pleating. Draw the front and back views of your design and suggest a suitable colour scheme and the types of material you would recommend. If you have time you may like to try out your top using paper or make it up in material to 1/4 scale.

LET'S LOOK AT TEXTILES IN THE HOME

VALUES
ENVIRONMENT INTERACTION
HEALTH
SAFETY
EFFICIENCY

Within our homes, textiles have come to play a very important role in fulfilling our need for comfort and well-being. Indeed, in some parts of the world actual 'homes' are built from textiles and natural material woven together to form shelters. Throughout history, the homes of the wealthy were made more comfortable by the use of textile hangings, floor coverings and upholstery. Today, we take it for granted that we have warm carpets and rugs on the floor, curtains to draw across the windows at night and attractively covered and upholstered furniture. We also take for granted the attractive 'extras' like lampshades, cushions and table linen.

AESTHETICS

Until fairly recently, people tended to furnish only once in a lifetime and younger people often inherited old pieces of furniture from their parents. Today, however, people are more inclined to plan their decor as a whole with everything matching and toning and following fashion for colours, patterns and shapes.

MAKING CHOICES

The types of fabric available, colours, textures and patterns are many and varied. Many shops specialise in supplying fabrics for interiors and often offer a complete 'design service' to include suggestions for colour schemes, furniture and accessories.

Shops such as *Next* and *Laura Ashley*, which started trading in fashion garments, now include furnishing sections offering 'collections' of fabrics, paints and accessories. In addition they sell fully illustrated catalogues of their goods shown in room settings which give the consumer a very good idea of how the materials, colours and patterns will look in the actual room. Often they provide a making-up service for curtains and loose covers too. If these ideas appeal and money is available, it is possible to convert a room or entire house or flat quickly, but not particularly cheaply, into a total environment.

Of course most people can neither afford such sweeping changes nor desire them and there are many ways in which new decorating ideas can be built up using existing items.

Choosing colour schemes for a family home may not be an easy matter as many more people will have to be considered or consulted. To some people the answer is to create mainly neutral backgrounds and so allow individuals to create their own 'space' by the inclusion of personal items.

KEY INVESTIGATION

ENVIRONMENT INTERACTION

Make a list of all the rooms in your home. You can do the survey even if you only have one room.
1. Remembering the broad definition of 'textiles', take each room in turn and list *all* the articles made from textiles that can be found there.

TEXTILES IN THE HOME

2 From your lists, put the articles into groups headed:
furniture
furnishings
sports/leisure equipment/toys
table linen
insulation
cleaning materials and equipment
decorative items
garage and car/bicycle/motor cycle

▷ **ANALYSIS**

VALUES
AESTHETICS
HEALTH
SAFETY

1 In which of these groups are textiles most used, and why?
2 How can we use textiles to enhance the appearance of our homes?
3 How do textiles contribute to the care of our homes?
4 How do textiles contribute to the making and serving of meals?
5 Comment on the current interest in 'keep fit' and say how textiles contribute to this trend.
6 How and why are textiles used in transport?

☐ **EVALUATION**

1 Why are textiles so important to us in our everyday lives?
2 Can you think of a substitute that could take their place? If not, why not?

In the choice and purchase of textiles for the home what practical considerations do you consider important?

Floor coverings: include carpets, rugs
Window coverings: include curtains, nets, blinds
Upholstery and loose covers
Bed linen
Table linen
Cleaning equipment and materials
Accessories: include lampshades, cushions

ENVIRONMENT INTERACTION

INVESTIGATION EXTENSION

Using an 'envelope' plan (see page 14) drawn to scale of your own room, design a new colour scheme to include furnishings and textile accessories. Collect suitable paint samples, fabric and carpet swatches. Mount these with descriptions on your design sheet.

▷ **ANALYSIS**

1 Calculate the cost of decorating the room.
2 Calculate the cost of fabrics needed for curtains, bed cover, etc.
3 Compare the cost of ready-made accessories with those you could make up yourself.

13

MAKING CHOICES

An envelope plan

☐ **EVALUATION**

What considerations did you take into account with regard to size, purpose and aspect?

In your opinion, how would the new decor enhance your room?

VALUES

In the matter of choices, the range of textiles available for clothing and home and family use is greater than ever before. As manufacturers and designers produce new and enticing ideas the average consumer might be excused for making some expensive mistakes.

However, the current attitude, particularly among the young, seems to be to enjoy a quick turnover of goods particularly in the field of clothing. With maturity and responsibility or a career and family, values change. It is important to recognise that we must all establish some practical guidelines for buying items such as those previously discussed and to try to foster discrimination in the choice of quality over quantity. Most people realise that 'value for money' is important but obviously the definition of this will change from person to person.

TECHNOLOGY

Generally, it can be seen that a knowledge of raw materials and characteristics of yarns, fabrics and fabric finishes is helpful and this, together with an understanding of design principles, can work to give a sound basis on which to make choices. However, personal likes and dislikes, instinct and the influences of friends and other influential people in our lives come into the matter too.

It is a balance of knowledge, personal feelings and experience which we 'pool' when the occasion arises to make a choice as a consumer.

The information and investigations which you have carried out have all been designed to help develop your interest in and your knowledge of textiles and to foster discrimination in their choice.

Fibres, Yarns and Fabrics

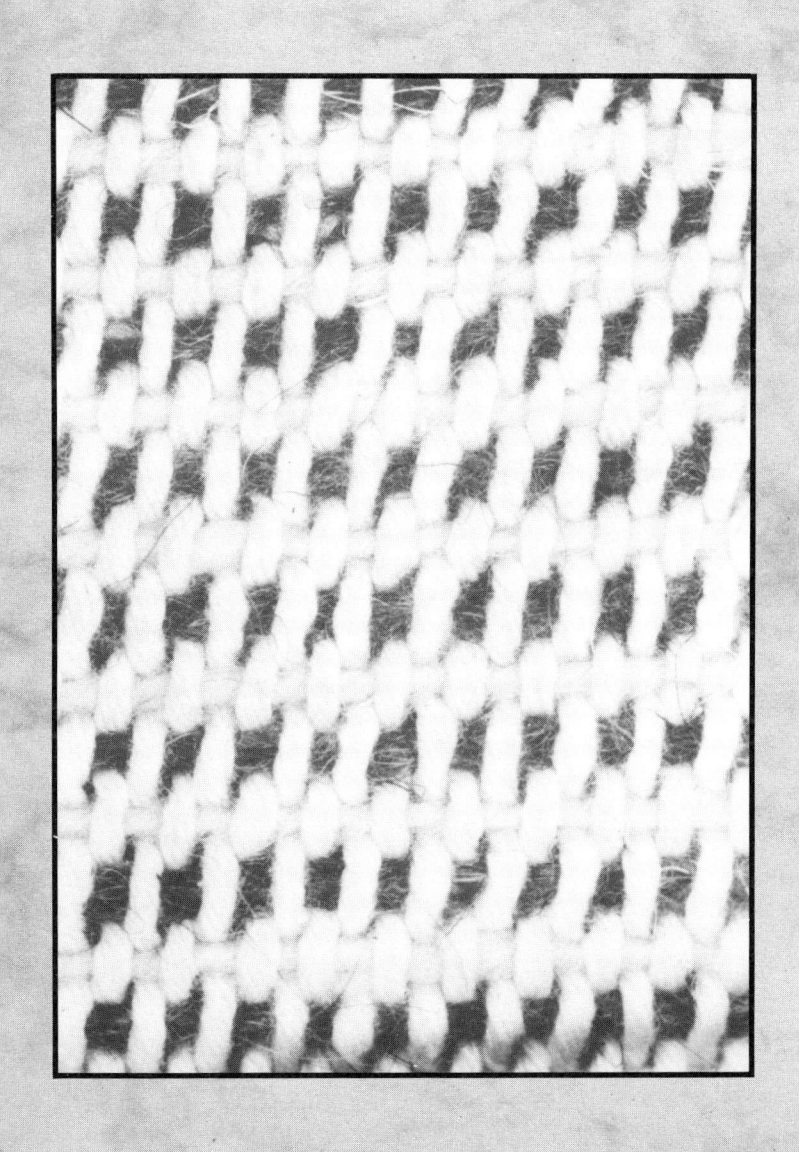

FIBRES, YARNS AND FABRICS

LET'S TAKE A CLOSE LOOK AT FABRICS

Early development

HUMAN DEVELOPMENT

As our ancestors started to travel and explore the known world, they discovered new countries, cultures and climates. One of the results of this exploration was that they brought back with them new and exciting raw materials and also finished lengths of fabric which they used for clothing or to decorate their homes.

People with a high social standing such as royalty, courtiers and wealthy landowners and merchants were able to acquire rich silks and other fine materials. Sometimes these were used for clothing on special occasions and sometimes for tapestries and wall-hangings which often depicted stories of journeys undertaken and battles won. Poorer people on the other hand whose lives were hard would have had none of these, the only textiles they would have would be rough, homespun and handwoven fabrics in wool, linen or cotton.

TECHNOLOGY

EFFICIENCY

The making of fabrics developed from these simple beginnings until the Industrial Revolution when, with the invention of steam power to drive machinery, handweaving virtually disappeared. During the 20th century, the textile industry has developed at a great pace. This has mainly been because of the introduction of new technology, scientific knowledge and the demands of the consumer society. The appearance of synthetic fibres has probably been the greatest development of all. This has resulted in many new, exciting fabrics which have almost replaced the more traditional ones which have been made and used for many centuries. However, recent trends have tended to combine the best of the old and the best of the new, thus bringing together the most useful properties of both.

Have a look at some of the labels inside your clothing and household textiles and you will discover how versatile these 'mixed' fibre fabrics are.

Natural fibres

ENVIRONMENT INTERACTION

As already indicated, the original fibres used were those from local plant and animal sources. Depending on the climatic conditions and social development of the people themselves these materials ranged from cotton and silk to camel and alpaca hair. As each culture developed differently, so did the development of textiles. Different tools and related skills produced colours and pattern in weaving and embroidery. Styles of clothing and different household articles, animal regalia, baskets and nets were all produced. Articles for everyday use and those for ceremonial and religious uses and also defence took on a distinctive appearance. It is fascinating to browse through the many fine exhibitions and collections that fill our museums and galleries showing textiles from the past. Many of these

HUMAN DEVELOPMENT

ancient textile articles are in excellent condition and give us an insight into the way of life of people from other lands and times.

Despite the wealth and variety of artefacts such as these, there are some common, underlying principles of design, structure and use which we have inherited and still use today despite the more sophisticated methods of production. It is the discovery, study and practice of these fundamental principles which we will be dealing with in this section.

KEY INVESTIGATION

Find out and list parts of the world where leaves and other plant materials and animal skins are still used for clothing and domestic purposes. Name the articles made and the plants and animals which provide the raw materials.

ANALYSIS

1. Do you think these materials are fit for their purpose? If so, why?
2. What factors create the environment where these natural materials are used?
3. What do you think would be the problems encountered in using skins for clothing?
4. Why are plant materials so useful in the building of simple houses?

EVALUATION

VALUES

How important do you think these natural materials are to the people who still use them?

Do you think they could be substituted by a modern, man-made product? If so, how?

INVESTIGATION EXTENSION

Find out how leather is produced.

Man-made fibres

Until comparatively recently only natural fibres were used to make fabrics. Commercial production of man-made fibres began in the 1920s. Today there are many man-made fibres in everyday use. These fall into two categories: regenerated and synthetic fibres.

FIBRES, YARNS AND FABRICS

Regenerated fibres have an animal (protein) or vegetable (cellulose) base, examples of fabrics made from these fibres are acetate, triacetate and viscose rayon.

Synthetic fibres are made entirely from chemicals and are usually derivatives from coal or oil. Nylon, polyester and acrylic are examples of synthetics.

TECHNOLOGY

During the last thirty years or so, fabrics made from man-made fibres have had a great impact on our way of life. Scientists have successfully developed fibres capable of replacing, improving on or blending with natural fibres and everyone has benefited from these developments. Man-made fibres have many qualities which natural fibres do not have and this is why they are in such demand, e.g. thermoplasticity—the ability to be moulded by heat. Water repellency and crease resistancy are other qualities.

Sometimes in fabrics these fibres are used alone, sometimes blended with natural fibres. This blending has many advantages as it combines the best properties of both types of fibre. A good example of this is polyester/cotton. Cotton alone is inclined to crease badly and needs careful ironing. Polyester alone does not absorb moisture, put the two together and you have a fabric which is virtually crease-resistant, washes easily and needs little ironing.

KEY INVESTIGATION

1 Look at the labels in the clothes you are wearing, find out what fibres have been used and present your findings in a table as shown below.

Garment	Natural fibre	Man-made fibre	Mixture	Wearability
Shirt or blouse			Polyester 50% Cotton 50%	Cool, easy to care for
Denim skirt or jeans	Cotton			Heavy
Socks or tights		Nylon		Hot and sticky

2 Look at as many household textile items as you can and make a similar table as before.

▷ ANALYSIS

1 *a* What % of your clothes are made from natural fibres?
   b What % of your clothes are made from man-made fibres?
   c What % of your clothes are made from a mixture of fibres?
2 Do the same analysis with the household articles you looked at.

Man-made fibres

Polyamide

Polyester

Acrylic

Natural fibres

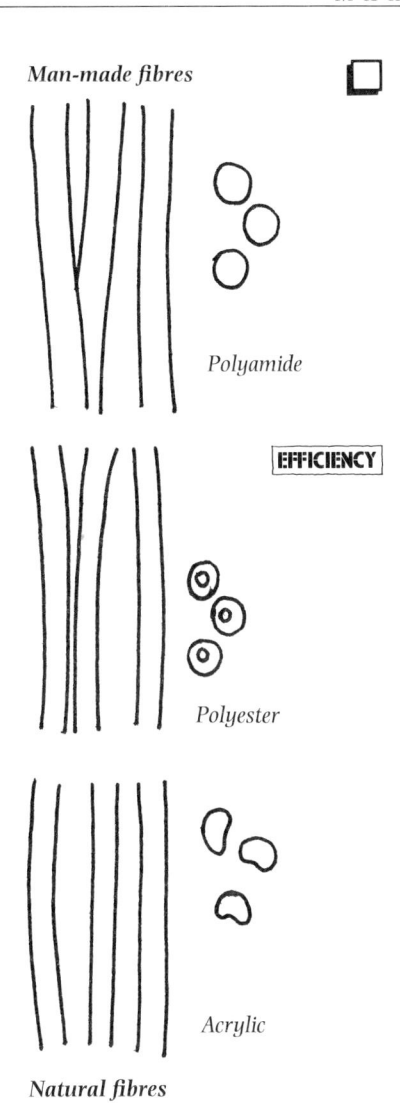

◻ **EVALUATION**

Look at the results of your investigations and analysis.
1. What impact has the production of man-made fibres had on the textile articles you examined?
2. Do you feel there is still a place for natural fibres? If so, why?
3. How do you rate the qualities of the fibre mixtures used in the textile articles you examined?

Making fibres into yarns

EFFICIENCY

All textiles are made from fibres. Some are short in length (staple) and some are continuous lengths (continuous filament). Most natural fibres are staple fibres and the lengths vary depending on the type of animal hair, the plant stems, leaves or seed hairs. Most man-made fibres are continuous filament fibres. These are invariably chopped up into shorter lengths before being spun. The exception is the naturally long filament obtained from the silk moth cocoon.

Natural fibres have their own distinctive colour, sometimes these are kept during processing such as in raw silk and Jacob sheep's wool. These natural colours have always been popular for certain types of articles but consumers do demand a broad range of colour choice. The dyeing process, which can take place at fibre, yarn or cloth stage is an important one and will be discussed later.

With very few exceptions, for example—raffia, a naturally tough plant material, all fibres go through the process which we know as spinning. This means the twisting together of a number of single fibres to form a thicker, stronger and more flexible yarn. It is this flexibility which makes textiles unique.

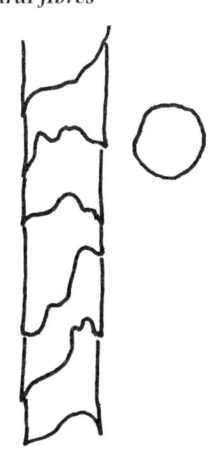

Wool fibres (animal hair) 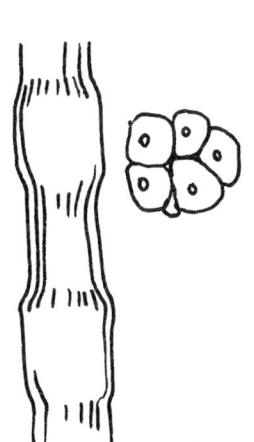   *Linen (plant stems)*   *Silk* 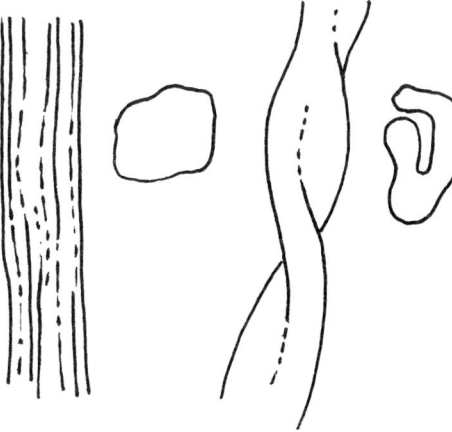   *Cotton (seed hairs)*

Twisted fibres forming yarn

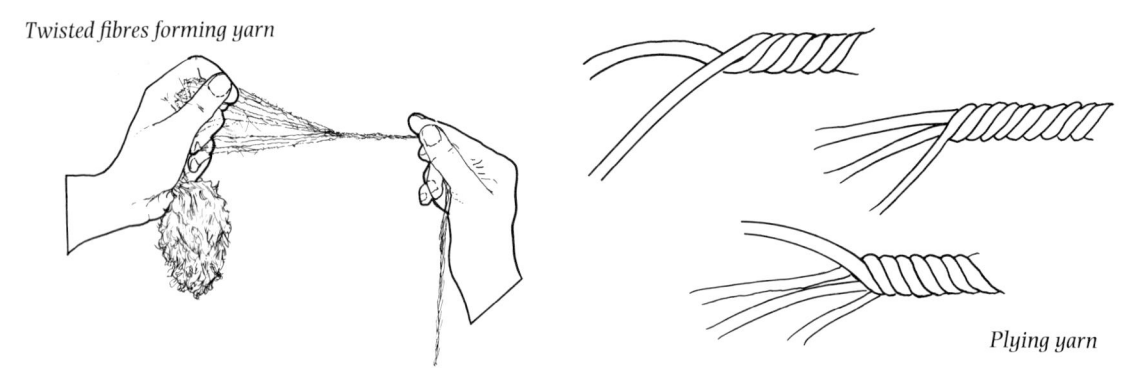

Plying yarn

Putting in a twist: making plain yarns

Try taking a few strands of sheep's wool in your fingers. You can often find some attached to a hedge or fence in the countryside. If it is teased out you will see its limitations, but put a twist in it and it immediately becomes a strong thread. By overlapping yet more fibres and twisting them in the same way as before, you will begin to extend the length of the yarn. This is the basic principle upon which all spinning began. This single twist of yarn has its own limitations, but by twisting it so much that it naturally springs back on itself, you will have made a '2 ply' yarn which is more than twice as strong as a single twisted yarn.

Any number of plies from 2 to 12 can be made but all these yarns are known as 'plain yarns'. They are easy to identify as they are always smooth and regular throughout their length. Most of the yarns which we use, from sewing cotton to yacht's ropes, are made in this way.

AESTHETICS

Interest can be achieved by twisting different coloured plies together, different thicknesses, and those of different types of fibres such as fluffy wool with firm cotton. Many interesting yarns may be created by this simple process and indeed, many of the varied knitting yarns available in the shops started life through this kind of experiment.

KEY INVESTIGATION

1. Make a collection of as many different plain yarns as you can find. Mount these and describe their use.
2. Try 'inventing' some yarns of your own by cutting up scrap materials, such as old nylon tights, rags, paper, plastic bags (particularly those with lettering), etc., and twisting them together.
   Knit up small samples using some of the yarns you make.
3. Try plying conventional and unconventional yarns together, one colour with another, thin with thick, rough with smooth, and so on. Be as inventive as you can.

▷ **ANALYSIS**

1 Describe fully the differences between the commercially produced yarns you found and those you made yourself.
2 Of those yarns you 'invented' which do you think might be used as
   a hand-knitting yarn
   b gift wrapping
   c decoration for the edge of a cushion
   d any other use.

☐ **EVALUATION**

In creative textiles, what advantages are there in making your own yarns?
What further work might you develop from your study of yarns?

INVESTIGATION EXTENSION

1 Make a list of all the crafts which depend on yarn as their basic raw material.
   Try some of these crafts for yourself using available resources.
2 Look in the shops and note the prices of macramé kits, knitting packs, etc. Try making up your own kit, perhaps to sell at a fund-raising event.
3 Having had some experience in handling a variety of yarns you should be able to put this to good use in the selection of materials for a collage panel. Try the following design brief.

Make a simple but richly-textured collage panel using some of the yarns you collected and invented. Use a linear theme like 'water patterns' or 'wood grain' as your starting point.

Fancy yarns

AESTHETICS   Sometimes called 'novelty yarns', these differ from plain yarns in a number of ways. In appearance, they have what look like knots, lumps and thin places along their length. They are more difficult to produce, require more technology and are therefore more expensive to buy. They are often weaker than plain yarns because they have thick and thin places which are not able to take strain equally along their length.

Possibly, the first fancy yarns made were produced by a person who could not hand-spin evenly and so produced yarn full of lumps and bumps! If you have ever tried spinning you will know it takes some time to develop the necessary skill to produce a free-flowing, regular yarn. The slight 'hiccups' produced when either too much or too little fibre is released through the fingers of the spinner will produce a knobbly or slubby appearance. These yarns can be put into identifiable categories.

Slub: yarn with thick and thin places.

Spiral or Gimp: combination of soft, thick yarn twisted with fine, hard yarn.

Bouclé: two different yarns are fed into the machine at different speeds, thus a wavy effect is produced.

Loop: stiff fibres (usually mohair) form loops which spring out of core yarn.

Snarl: very highly twisted yarn.

Knop: ground yarn is held under tension as knops build up at a fast speed.

Chenille: a woven cut fabric yarn.

There are numerous other ways of producing fancy yarns, some simple, some more complex. Something you could try yourself is to space dye a hank of plain yarn such as dishcloth cotton.

> **Space dyed yarn**
> To do this, take a length of cotton yarn, like dishcloth cotton and first wash it to ensure good dye penetration. Arrange it in a hank by winding it over a piece of card or over the back of a chair. Lightly tie the hank in a few places to avoid the yarn tangling. Make up some small quantities of dyes in two or three colours. Drape part of the hank in the first dye, another part in a second dye and so on. Leave for the required amount of time. Remove hank of yarn and rinse carefully.

Most of the fancy yarns described on page 22 are used in the weaving of fabric as weft yarns. Generally, they are not strong enough to form a warp. In machine knitting, they tend to snag in the fine needle hooks but are being developed continuously as hand-knitting yarns. (For warp and weft see page 26.)

AESTHETICS

The fabric produced by the use of fancy yarns will have an interesting surface texture. In weaving, the finer slub yarns produce attractive fabric for use in dresses, trousers, skirts and jackets. The more exaggerated such as knop and chenille yarns are extensively used in upholstery materials.

As already mentioned, hand-knitting yarns are one of the chief outlets for much of the fancy yarn produced. Most of us own a thick knit sweater in a knobbly texture, indeed, much of the lovely casual wear for summer which has become so popular, is knitted in these yarns in soft or strong colours.

TECHNOLOGY

Due to their popular demand in clothing, knitting machines, both domestic and industrial, have had to be developed to take these fancy yarns.

KEY INVESTIGATION

1. Collect samples of fancy yarns and examine them through a hand lens. Mount your samples and identify them then make a sketch of the structure of each.
2. If possible, make a visit to a local shop selling knitting yarns and have a look at the variety available and the patterns produced for the fancy yarns, note prices also.
   Bring in some items of knitwear to study. Look at the yarns through a hand lens.
3. Try inventing some fancy yarns of your own. Use some cheap plain yarns and knot, twist, plait, finger crochet or knit them.
   Mount your samples and explain how you achieved the result.

FIBRES, YARNS AND FABRICS

▷ **ANALYSIS**

1. Which types of yarn are
   - *a* most commonly used?
   - *b* least commonly used?
   - *c* your own favourites?

   Give your reasons.
2. Compare the prices of the different types of fancy yarns.
3. Describe fully the differences between the commercially produced yarns and those you invented yourself.

☐ **EVALUATION**

1. Why do you think there is such a demand for fancy yarns?
2. Do you think the effect of using fancy yarns in knitwear justifies the higher prices?
3. Having had some experience in handling fancy yarns and seeing their effects in knitwear you should be able to carry out the following design brief.

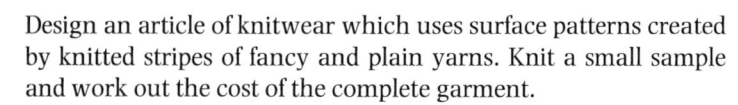

   Design an article of knitwear which uses surface patterns created by knitted stripes of fancy and plain yarns. Knit a small sample and work out the cost of the complete garment.

INVESTIGATION EXTENSION

1. On a square of card 20 cm × 20 cm draw a sweater shape—you can do this free-hand or if you can find one that fits trace it from a picture or knitting pattern. Cut out the shape and discard it but keep the frame. Take some colour supplement magazine sheets and place the frame over different areas of pictures until you find a pleasing pattern. Cut out the piece of coloured picture and stick it carefully behind your frame. Do this exercise several times and mount all your designs on one sheet or in a sketch book.

   From your collection of fancy yarns, suggest suitable yarns and colour schemes for your designs. Stick yarn samples close to your designs.

2. Find a picture of a landscape, seascape, seaweed, root-formation, or interesting sky. Using knitting, crochet, wrapping, tassels, pom-poms, etc., translate your picture into a textural collage. You will find that some threads may suggest ideas to you or you can create areas of texture using any suitable techniques:

   e.g. coarse brown yarn—the bark of a tree,
   white mohair yarn—clouds,
   shaded green yarn—fields.

   Mount your completed work.

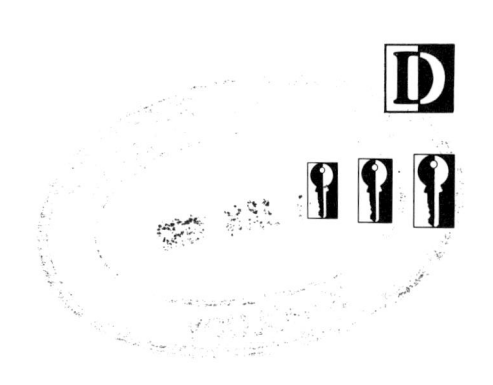

LET'S LOOK AT FABRIC STRUCTURES

TECHNOLOGY

Possibly the most ancient form of fabric construction is the process of weaving. Knitted textiles are also ancient in origin and have become more versatile in recent years since the development of high powered knitting machines. In addition, other textile constructions such as felting (see page 34) have origins in the distant past and have been updated to provide many of the 'non-wovens' that are in common use today in clothing, household and industrial textiles like carpet underlay, household cleaning cloths and hats. Because of the fragile nature of textiles made in the past from natural materials, there are very few actual examples left from the very early days of fabric-making. However, we can study illustrations of people weaving on primitive looms which appear on pottery such as that from ancient Greece. Wall-paintings from the civilisation of ancient Egypt also show what a variety of fabrics were used for the making of clothing for both slave and Pharaoh.

Woven fabrics

As previously stated, weaving is a very ancient art which has its origin in times unknown. We know that possibly the first woven structures were in fact simple shelters made from plant material.

25

FIBRES, YARNS AND FABRICS

Woven fencing today perhaps perpetuates this method. In addition, baskets were made from both firm and soft plant materials which of course, are still widely used today for both practical and decorative purposes. The principle of weaving, that is interlacing one set of strands in and out of another was found to produce practical, flexible material. Depending on whether the strands are fine and strong like linen, or short and stiff like willow twigs, a tremendous number of textiles with differing characteristics and uses can be made.

EFFICIENCY

Besides the basic principles of the interlacing of warp and weft the other common element which links all forms of weaving is the equipment needed to produce it. This is known as a loom and its function is the same, whether it is a simple one such as might be used by primary school children or a highly sophisticated computer-operated power loom such as might be seen in a modern weaving factory.

> Weaving takes place when a group of parallel yarns set up in a vertical position (the warp) are interlaced by another set of yarns running in a horizontal direction (the weft). Warp yarns are called ends and rows of weft are known are picks.

EFFICIENCY

The primary function of a loom is to hold the warp threads evenly under tension and to regulate the space between them. There then needs to be some means of beating the rows of weaving down to form a firm cloth. In addition, there must be a device which carries the weft threads through the warp. This is known as a shuttle. Generally,

Tree loom

WOVEN FABRICS

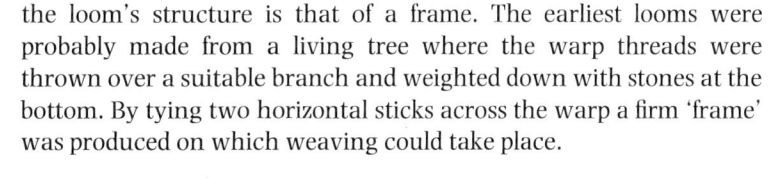

the loom's structure is that of a frame. The earliest looms were probably made from a living tree where the warp threads were thrown over a suitable branch and weighted down with stones at the bottom. By tying two horizontal sticks across the warp a firm 'frame' was produced on which weaving could take place.

The problem with this type of loom is that it is fixed in one position and is therefore not portable, making its use limited, particularly in bad weather!

An improvement on this type of loom was the making of a free standing frame basically constructed from four pieces of wood. These types of looms are still used in many parts of the world. Simple looms like these can easily be made from readily available materials like strong card, hardboard or ply scraps, a few nails or cup hooks and pieces of dowelling.

Two simple looms which you might consider making for yourselves are:

- Frame loom—you will need: a wooden frame, pieces of dowelling and four cup hooks.

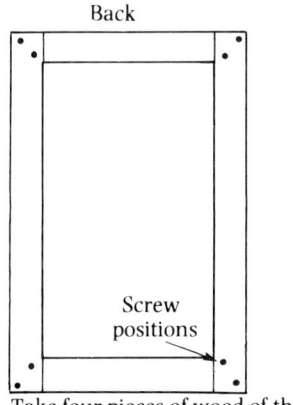

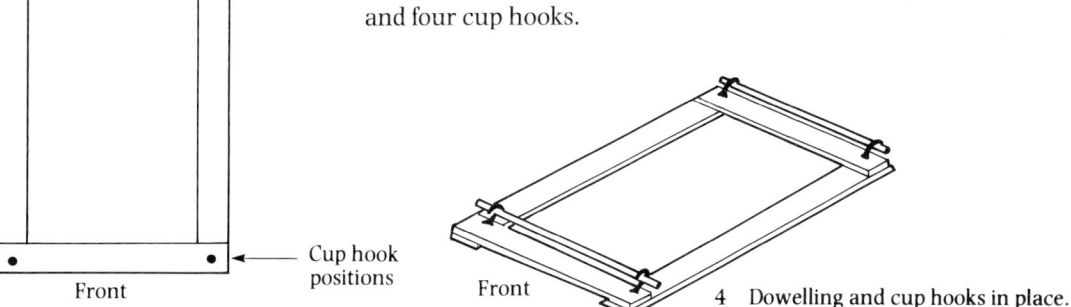

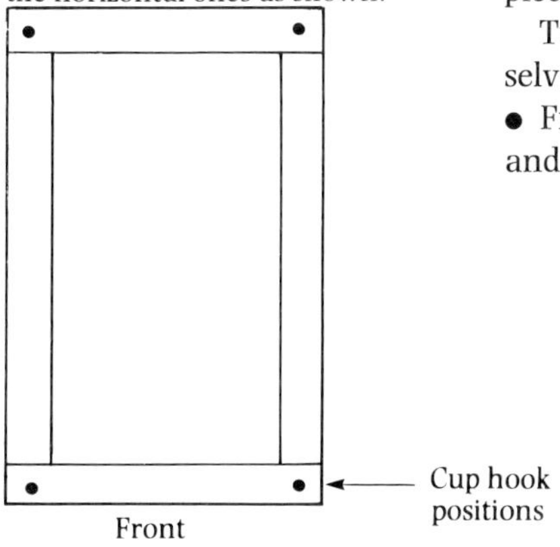

1 Take four pieces of wood of the required length.
2 Screw the vertical pieces over the horizontal ones as shown.
3 Put cup hooks in place as shown.
4 Dowelling and cup hooks in place.

Frame loom

- Backstrap loom—this loom actually uses the weaver's body as part of its structure.

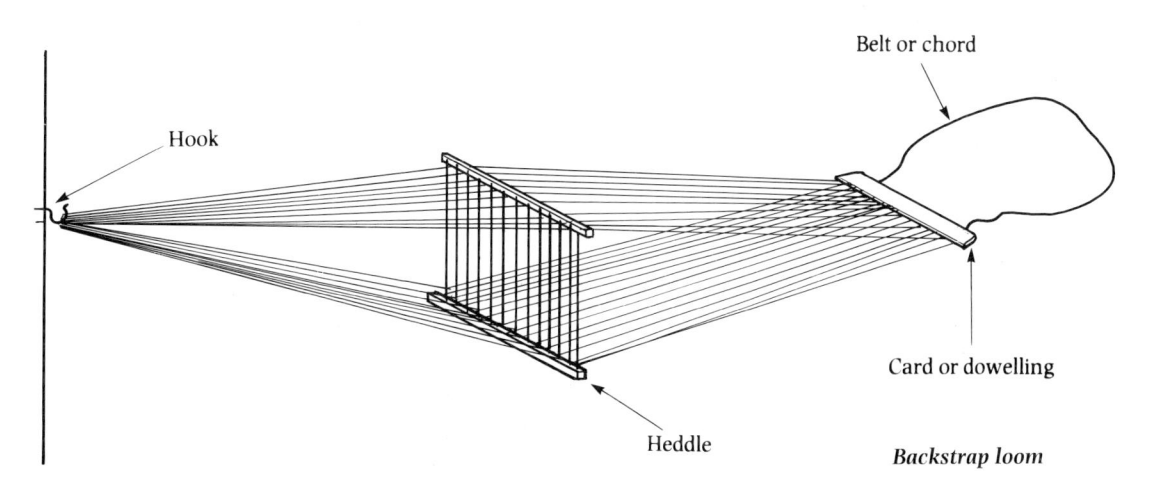

Backstrap loom

27

You will need: cardboard to make a heddle (see below), dowelling and warp yarn.

It is possible to buy a number of simple looms ready made or in kit form from craft suppliers.

Backstrap loom

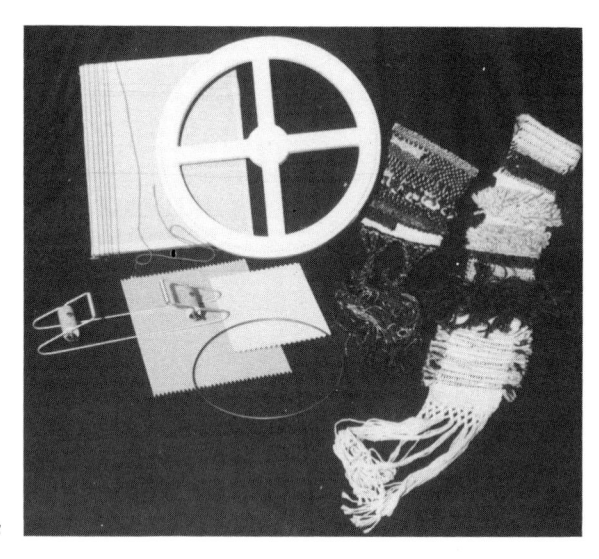

Commercially produced hand looms

EFFICIENCY

TECHNOLOGY

The next stage towards the modern looms that we know today was the production of roller looms. These had a 'comb-like' attachment known as a heddle through which the warp strands could be threaded and, at the back and front of the loom, rounded pieces of wood made into adjustable rollers. The problem of limited warp length which occurred with the previously described looms was thus overcome. Lengths of warp thread could be wound on to the back roller and as fabric was woven by means of a shuttle carrying the weft yarn, it could be rolled on to the front roller.

The use of rollers (back and front), a heddle, a shuttle and a device for beating the rows of weaving down (known as a reed), completed the mechanical needs of making fabric at some speed. This has become the principle on which all modern looms are based.

Looms were originally operated entirely by hand, but eventually foot-powered looms were developed, then steam-powered looms and today most are electrically operated. The shuttle can now be operated by a 'hammer-like' mechanism, powerful jets of water or compressed air.

If you get an opportunity, visit a modern weaving complex. It is well worth seeing and guided tours are available at most by appointment. If not, try to make contact with a local handweaver who will usually be delighted to arrange for small groups to visit.

The history of the development of the loom and the weaving industry is a fascinating story, bringing in social and economic as well as technological changes. Nevertheless, there are still many craftsmen/women today who work on simple equipment to produce beautiful, original fabrics. Again, it is worth visiting a craft workshop or watching a demonstration to see a 'fine art' weaver in action.

KEY INVESTIGATION

1. Using available resources warp up a suitable simple loom such as a card or frame type. Use strong, medium-weight yarn of about 4 ply thickness.
2. Using available resources, work stripes of at least 2 cm each of plain weave, tapestry weave, sumak and rya knotting. These latter techniques will add surface interest to your work.

ANALYSIS

Using a table such as the one shown below, describe the effects that were produced by the different weave patterns.

Yarn	Weave	Effect
Plain, double knitting wool	Tapestry	Solid, smooth texture

EVALUATION

From the results of your investigation into different weave patterns what do you consider:
1. the most suitable yarn(s) for tapestry weave and why;
2. the most suitable yarn(s) for plain weave and why;
3. the most suitable yarn(s) for sumak weave and why;
4. the most suitable yarn(s) for rya knotting and why?

Overall, what is the most versatile yarn for handweaving?

INVESTIGATION EXTENSION

AESTHETICS

Design on paper a small scale tapestry panel based on the idea of 'strata'. Plan a colour scheme and stick on samples of suitable yarns for each area.

Work the tapestry, remove it from the loom and decide on a suitable method of finishing off the piece of work. Complete the tapestry and write a short passage to describe what you have learnt about the following:
1. Relationship of plain and fancy yarns with chosen weave pattern.
2. Method of starting and finishing off yarns.
3. Time taken to produce tapestry.

FIBRES, YARNS AND FABRICS

Weave patterns in commercially produced textiles

By carrying out an extensive study of handweaving equipment and weave patterns you will have discovered for yourself the principles of weaving and the nature of the equipment needed to produce woven fabric. Today, most of the fabric used for everyday purposes is produced by this same process. Plain weave and its variations are the most frequently used, with twill weaves and satin weaves used for more specialised effects. Illustrations of these are shown here.

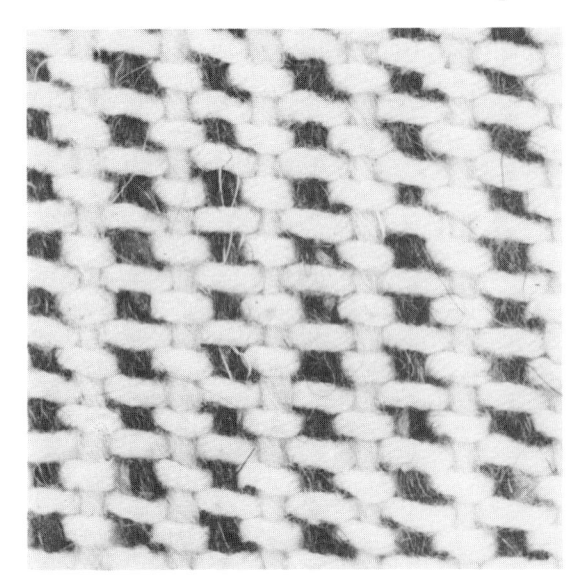

(Left) Plain weave
(Right) Twill weave

KEY INVESTIGATION

Your teacher will supply you with a number of named samples of fabric on which the warp direction should be marked. You will need a hand lens and a large needle.
1. Examine each sample carefully, unravelling a few rows of weft to expose the warp yarns.
2. Identify the weave pattern.
3. Identify the types of yarn used.
4. Study the colour of both warp and weft yarns.

ANALYSIS

1. Assess the thickness (weight) of the yarns used and their texture. Describe these, and relate to the weight of the fabric.
2. Assess the way in which the weave patterns affect the handle (feel) of each fabric.
3. Assess the use of colour of both the individual yarns used in each fabric and the overall effect they give when woven into fabric.

KNITTED FABRICS

☐ EVALUATION

As a result of your investigations, sketch an article (clothing or household) which you feel would be suitably made from each of your sample fabrics. Put sketches and sample fabrics together to create a design sheet or mount them in your sketch book or folder.

INVESTIGATION EXTENSION

Using 1 cm wide paper strips in two or more colours, experiment with plain and twill weaves to create checks and stripes. The better results can be recreated in felt and made up into small articles such as pencil cases.

Knitted fabrics

As with woven textiles, little is actually known about the exact origin of knitting. It is said that Joseph's coat of many colours was knitted. The first knitting was done on single or pairs of sharpened sticks (needles) and surprisingly the first knitting machine was invented in the 16th century.

EFFICIENCY

The process differs from weaving in that it is built up of interlocking loops formed by a single strand of yarn. In weaving, you will remember, two separate sets of yarn are required—warp and weft.

Knitting as most of us know it is performed by hand on two needles and is known as weft knitting. A row of loops (stitches) are put on one needle and the fabric is formed as the second needle pulls the yarn through each loop individually to form a new row of stitches.

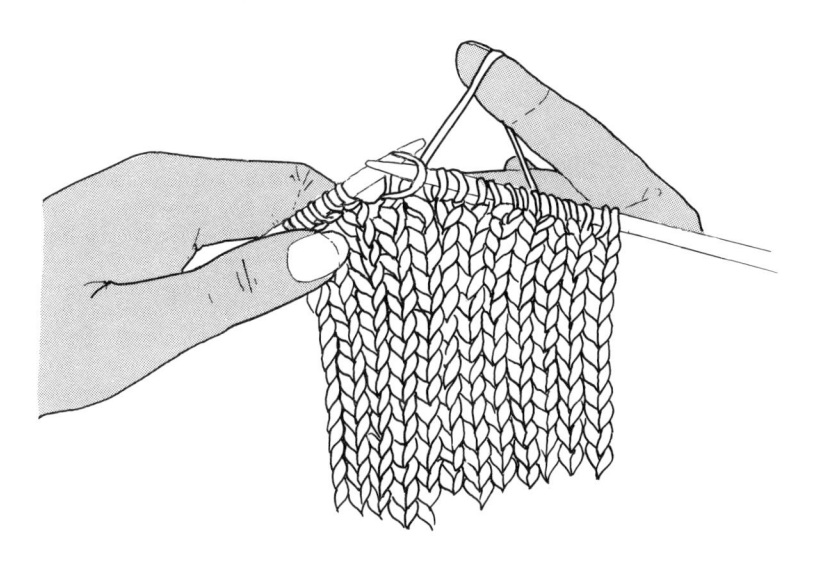

FIBRES, YARNS AND FABRICS

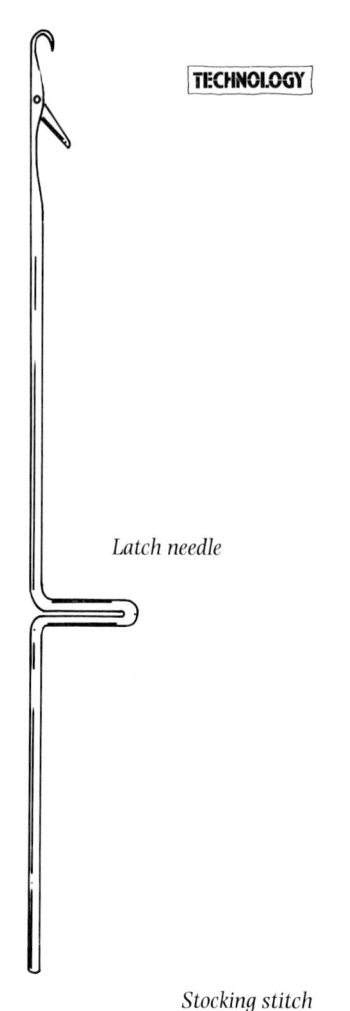

TECHNOLOGY

In machine knitting, however, there is one needle for every stitch. These needles are generally 'latch' needles and it is the action of the 'latch' which pulls the yarn through the old loop to form a new stitch. Domestic knitting machines are flat bed machines but industry uses both flat and circular knitting machines. In the 18th century, a process known as 'warp' knitting was invented whereby each needle had a separate thread, the loops being interlocked vertically. A 'beard' needle is more commonly used on these machines.

Plain knit fabric The simplest knitted fabric is made with all the loops intermeshing in the same direction. In hand knitting this is known as stocking stitch. The front or face of the fabric is smooth and looks like a series of 'Vs'. The back or reverse of the fabric is rough and looks like interlocked semicircles.

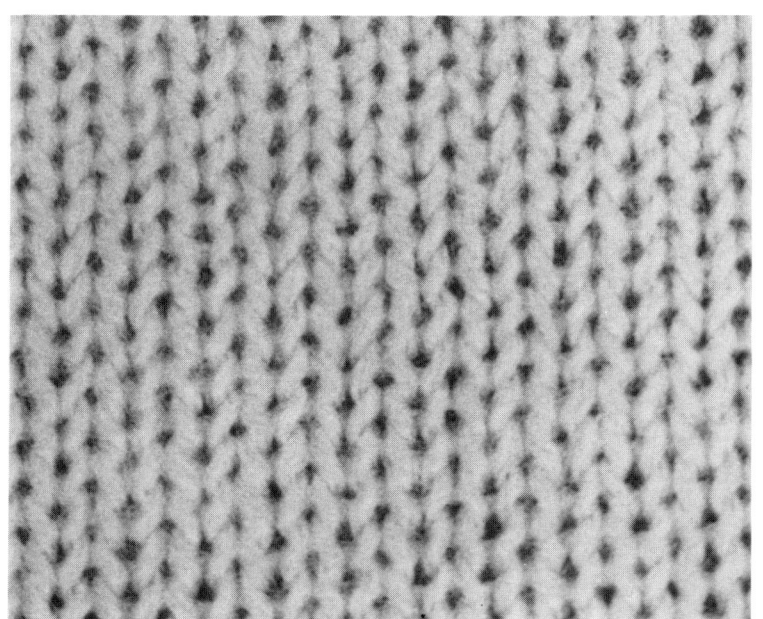

Latch needle

Stocking stitch

Plain knit structures are used for most of the knitted fabric we use. Each row of knitting is known as a course and each vertical line formed is known as a wale.

Rib fabric In hand knitting, this is produced by alternately knitting into the front of one stitch and the back of the next (knitting a plain stitch and then a purl stitch). Machine-knitted rib fabrics are knitted on two sets of needles. There are many variations on rib fabric. The one described is known as 1 × 1 rib (one stitch plain one stitch purl) but it is possible to knit 2 × 2 rib or 1 × 2 rib or 3 × 3 rib depending on the result required. Rib knitting has good stretch (elasticity) and is often used for the welts and cuffs of jumpers.

KNITTED FABRICS

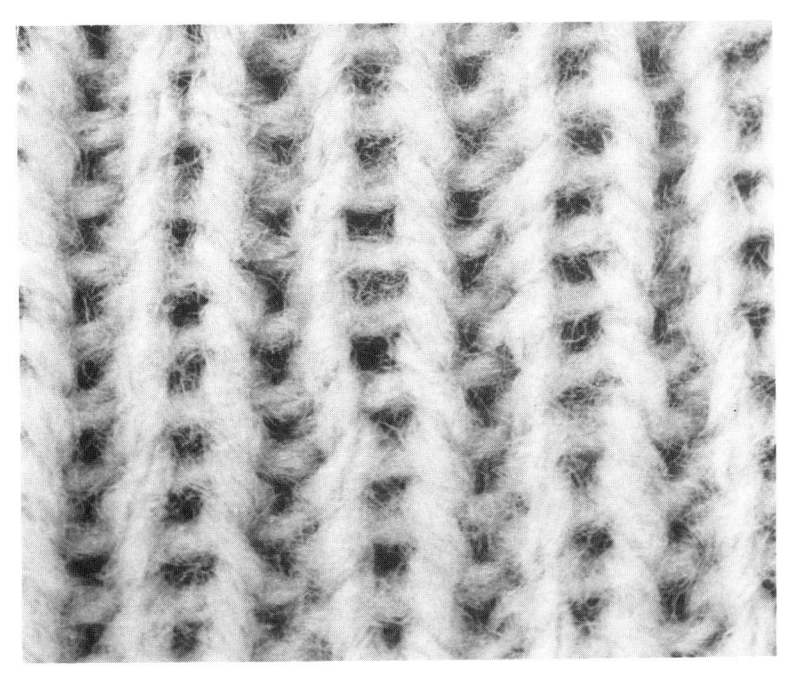

1 × 1 rib

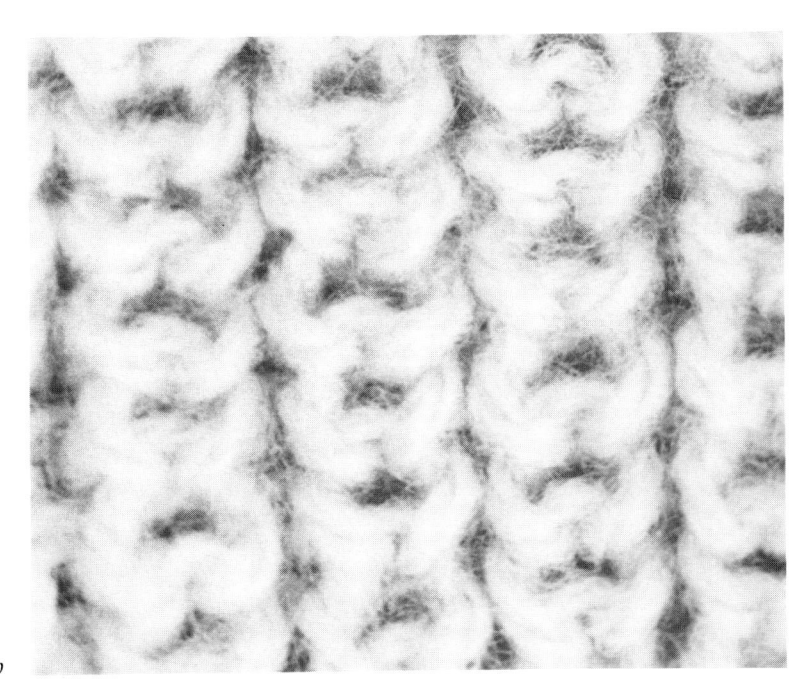

Fisherman's rib

Tuck stitch fabrics   It is useful to note these fabrics as they have a thicker, heavier appearance than those previously mentioned. They are less 'elastic' too. Various tuck stitch effects can produce open work, lacy fabrics and surface texture. In hand knitting the simplest form is known as fisherman's rib.

Felted and bonded fabrics

We will all be familiar with both these types of textile but often a knowledge of their manufacture is less well known. The making of felt ranks with weaving and knitting as one of the oldest forms of textile structure. It is said that the original felt was made by accident. Nomadic tribesmen walking long distances with their flocks of sheep put wads of wool into their sandals to make them more comfortable. The combination of heat, sweat and pressure compacted the wool into a firm pad. This we know as felt and it is from wool and wool blends that felt is still made today.

We tend to think of felt as a craft material, a non-fraying, colourful, soft and matt surfaced fabric. It is also an extremely versatile material being used as carpet underlay, in upholstery, and has many industrial uses.

When wetted, the scales on wool fibres stand away and if the water is hot, the fibre shrinks. Combining heat and moisture with pressure makes the fibres cling together to form a dense web.

In earlier times, felt was used as protection for the body against the cold and against weapons of war. These garments usually took the form of jerkins, cloaks, hats, leggings and footwear. Felt was also used for saddle cloths, floor coverings and, of course, tents. So a material which had such humble beginnings was eventually used for human shelter. Pure wool felt is today a very expensive material and is often used for fashionable hats because it can be moulded into many different shapes.

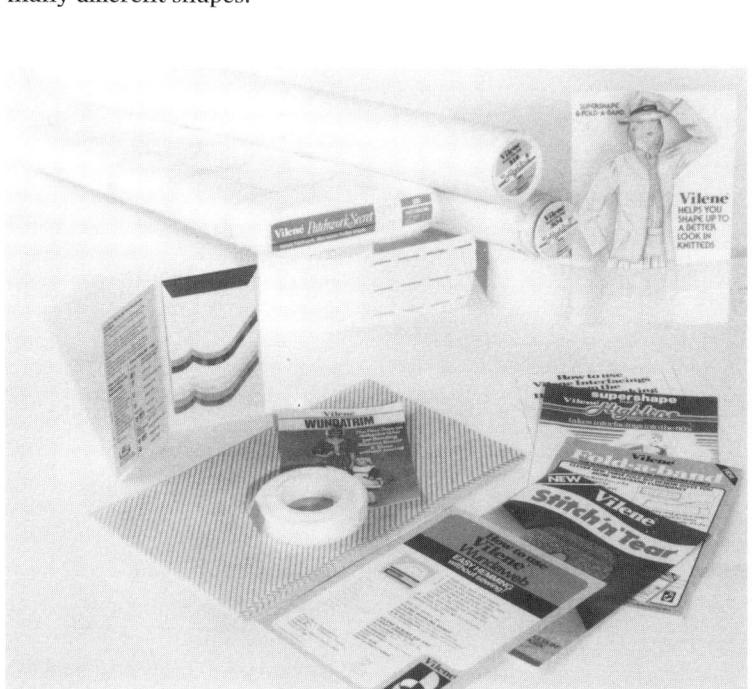

Bonded iron-on materials

FELTED AND BONDED FABRICS

TECHNOLOGY

By contrast, bonded fabrics are new and have appeared only since the arrival of man-made fibres. These textiles are made from short lengths of fibre, arranged in a criss-cross fashion in layers which are then 'bonded' together with resin.

The most commonly recognised bonded fabrics are those used for interfacing (stiffening areas of garments such as collars) and those used as household cleaning cloths.

Some of the more recent developments in the manufacture and use of bonded fabrics concern the addition of an adhesive. This enables the material to be 'ironed on' to the fabric it is there to support. Bonded iron-on materials are now sold in a number of forms, each one being specially made for a specific job.

KEY INVESTIGATION

1. Collect small samples (5 cm × 5 cm) of different types of bonded and felted textiles that have been provided.
   Examine each with a hand lens and dissect a part of each from one edge using a long needle.
2. Mount each sample and give a full description. Include a diagram and the price of each type of fabric as shown below.

Sample	Structure	Description	Use	Size/Width	Price
A		Bonded, lightweight, open texture, yellow and white stripes	All purpose household cloth	36 cm × 60 cm	25 in packet @

ANALYSIS

Using only three of the bonded interfacing samples that you have previously examined, iron or stitch these on to the following samples of fabric:
1. fine woven cotton or polyester cotton fabric;
2. knitted sweatshirt fabric;
3. medium or heavyweight tweed fabric.

Method

1. Cut your fabric pieces into four pieces, put one piece of each aside as a control.
2. On each of the other three pieces, either iron on or stitch in the different types of interfacing provided.
3. Compare each sample in turn with the appropriate control. Note changes in thickness, stiffness, flexibility, stretch. Tabulate your results.

FIBRES, YARNS AND FABRICS

EVALUATION

1. From your investigations, what do you think are the advantages of modern bonded textiles?
2. Discuss the advantages and disadvantages of sew-in and iron-on interfacings.

Design and make a small article in felt which shows off its colour and texture and its non-fraying characteristics to advantage. For example, you could make a pin cushion, Christmas tree decoration or key ring fob.

INVESTIGATION EXTENSION

1. On a suitable background, e.g. tie-dyed fabric, spray-dyed fabric or fabric crayoned background, stick or stitch some cut-out figures or objects in felt to form a silhouette against your chosen background.

    Suggested themes may be:
    The Three Wise Men;
    A wagon train;
    Skyline of tall buildings.

2. Felt can be cut easily and the material manipulated in the fingers into different shapes and textures because of its non-fraying qualities. For example, it can be rolled, twisted, folded, pleated, gathered, etc.

Using scraps of felt, design and make a landscape or cityscape, no larger than 20 cm × 30 cm, using the methods described above. You may have to stitch some of the pieces into place because adhesives are difficult to use on small felt pieces.

Design Matters

LET'S LOOK AT DESIGN

AESTHETICS

When we look around the shops at the vast array of goods for sale, it is important to remember that every one of them has been designed.

Design is a fundamental process through which everything we use has come about. It is not achieved as some might think by a group of artists who are suddenly inspired 'to design'. The process of design is a lengthy one and involves many people of different talents, skills and knowledge. Design takes place as a response to a consumer need, and is based on 'problem-solving' processes.

EFFICIENCY

In textiles, as with many other products, professional designers are only one part of the story. Design must be 'managed' and this involves teams or groups of people within a company or group of companies, working together to think out, produce and sell the finished product. This involves market research design, appropriate manufacturing processes, marketing and retailing.

The article may be a 'one-off' or more likely these days, to be one of an integrated range of products, such as mix and match fashion separates or as mentioned previously a co-ordinated range of fabrics, furnishing and accessories as sold in shops like *Next, Marks & Spencer* and *Laura Ashley*.

Evolution of a textile design: a beach towel

It might be helpful to study the progress of a textile product from the drawing board through to the point of sale. If we are planning to buy an article like a towel, it is surprising what choice we have. Looking around the shops or market stalls we will find large beach towels, sports towels, bath and hand towels, towels for babies, towels for presents. It is interesting to note what a great choice the consumer has and to ask oneself 'how do I make that choice?' The factors that help us to make up our minds depend largely on the design of the towel. Most people would not give any consideration to the idea of design and would probably be persuaded by colour, size, softness, or price.

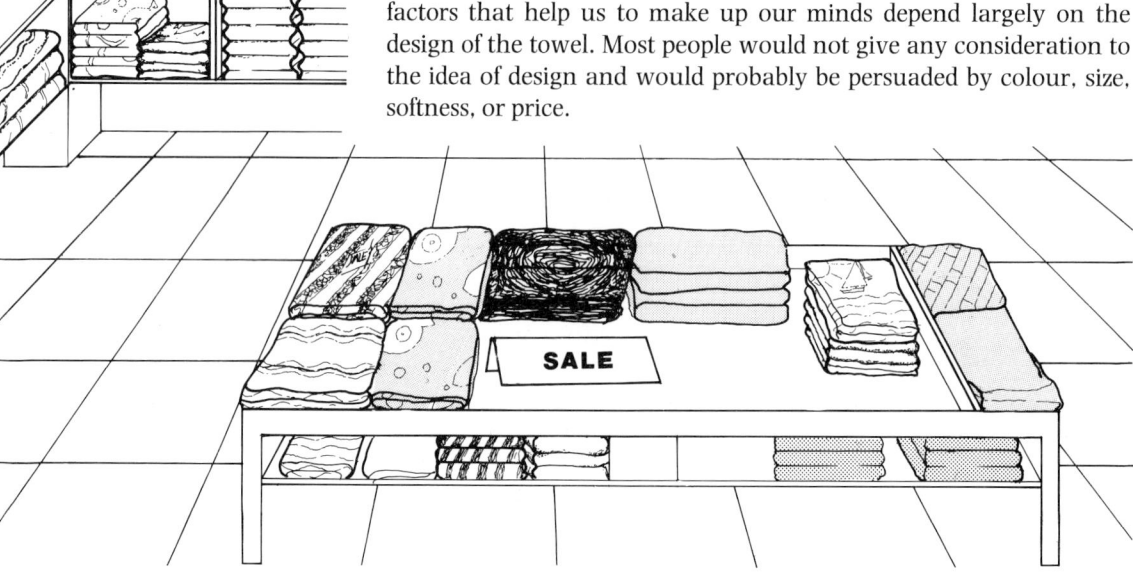

However, all these elements are actually design considerations and it is these and others that we will go on to look at.

Design in textiles therefore, is not just the colour or shape or decoration of the article, but includes much more.

Firstly, let's look at designers themselves. It might be thought that only one person working in a design studio attached to the particular company produces the design. In fact finished designs, such as for our towel, start many years before the product appears in the shops, and involve a great many people.

As we are all aware, colour in particular is one of the first things we notice about any new article we may be about to buy. Groups of people, known as 'colourists' actually start work on planning new colours and combinations of colour at least two years in advance of the range being seen in the shops. Recently, a great deal more interest in colour has been shown by the general public. Most shops set out their goods, whether it be paints and wallpapers, kitchenware or articles of clothing into colour 'families'. This makes it easier for customers to identify the colours that please them and thus make their choice of purchase much easier.

Flowers have always been a popular motif for items of household textiles, it might be that exotic flowers are considered or the group might feel these have been used too many times before.

AESTHETICS

Often a 'brainstorming session' will be held. The group will produce a list of ideas that remind them of the sea—buckets and spades, fish, seaweed, boats, and so on. These may be obvious ideas but the team would probably then go on to slightly more unusual ideas or indeed, some bizarre ones!

Colour will also be discussed—traditionally towels for the home were in pale pastel colours and for the beach, dark colours which did not show the dirt were used. More recently, bright primary and secondary colours have become fashionable. Consumers are also known to want to buy towels that match their swimwear so perhaps these would have been researched.

Let us say that the design team agree to try a range of beach towels in bold animal prints of stripes and spots using 'jungle' colours. The next stage is to sketch out some ideas for these on paper to a small scale. Many hundreds of little coloured sketches might be produced by one or two team members. Some might be drawn up to half or quarter scale.

They would have to consider the sizes and proportions of their towels and how they would be finished off, e.g. with a fringe or hem. They might also consider any additional articles that could be produced in the same range.

Another meeting of the design team would then have to be called so that everyone could look at the ideas being put forward. In this instance, people involved in the technical side of production would need to be present to discuss the practicalities of the design (remember, towels have to be double-sided, the design being reversed on the back).

TECHNOLOGY

In addition, someone from the marketing department would need to advise on launching times, costing and advertising of the articles.

The designers themselves would need then to draw up more positive plans for the range. Computer aided design (CAD) might be used. On a computer, ideas for designs can be stored and variations such as changes in scale, proportion and colour might be produced by the operator. The computer print out can produce sections of the design in colour which can be seen in full scale. This operation is a great time-saver and gives the design team a very good idea of what the finished towels will look like. More detail of this operation is given in Section 5.

Once approved, the next stage takes the towel design into the hands of the weaver who will set up a loom to produce a trial run of the designs. These will then be assessed and any faults remedied before further progress is made. More meetings need to be held to ensure that everyone concerned is happy with the finished ideas and then the job of selling the product begins.

We must not forget the importance of packaging the product once it is made. The design of this is another important stage in the process.

The marketing team will know its potential customers and will launch the product as necessary with publicity in the form of advertising in magazines, newspapers, posters and hand-outs. Once the product reaches the shops, the window dressers and store designers display the range and the towels will hopefully catch the eye of the potential customer.

EVOLUTION OF A TEXTILE DESIGN

KEY INVESTIGATION

Select either **A** or **B**.

A From home, bring a textile article, such as a duvet cover, which has been bought recently from a well-known shop or store (not a market).
   Working in pairs:
examine the article in detail from the point of view of its design, make notes on the following:
1. Size/shape,
2. Colour,
3. Texture,
4. Surface pattern, if any.

ANALYSIS

VALUES

Good design should be a balance of function and performance with visual appeal. Individually, answer the following questions:
1. Do you consider your article to be well designed or not?
   Make a list of points that support your answer.
2. Do you consider your articles were good value for money?
   Compare your answers and ideas with those of your partner.

EVALUATION

Imagine you are shopping for a new version of the article you investigated. List the design points that you would be looking for. Write a short paragraph that could be used in a magazine advertisement which tells potential consumers that the product is well designed.

B Bring your favourite jacket, anorak or coat from home. Examine the article once again from the point of view of design.
   Working in pairs:
make notes on the following:
1. Size/shape (include shape of sleeves and collar),
2. Colour,
3. Texture,
4. Whether it has any trimming,
5. Whether it is reversible—what changes there are to its appearance.

▷ **ANALYSIS**

Analyse the garment by asking yourself the following questions:
1 Do you consider your article to be well designed or not? Make a list of points that support your answer.
2 Do you consider your articles were good value for money? Compare your answers and ideas with those of your partner.

◻ **EVALUATION**

Imagine that you are shopping for a new version of the garment you investigated. List the design points that you would be looking for. Write a short paragraph that could be used in a magazine advertisement which informs potential consumers that the garment is well designed.

The Design Council

The Design Council is a government-funded organisation which helps promote good design. It deals with all consumer goods from cars to teaspoons. Until recently a distinctive seal of approval was awarded to well-designed products which met the Council's criteria for good design. This could be used on labels, advertisements, etc. The Council has its headquarters in London's Haymarket where there is always a display of recently approved goods including textiles.

To achieve the Design Council's approval, the following criteria had to be met.

The product had to be:
- well made,
- easy to use,
- suited to its purpose,
- simple to maintain,
- good looking,
- value for money.

In addition, products had to meet relevant UK safety standards.

As you can see, visual appearance is only one of the elements looked for as regards 'good' design. Too many people are swayed only by appearances when they are shopping and do not consider other qualities important. This attitude has led to many articles being produced of a poor standard, which in turn leads to customer dissatisfaction and problems.

It is necessary for every consumer to be aware of what design is, how it affects the goods we buy and why we must try to appreciate the qualities of good design.

To do this, it is useful to design something yourself. Design is about solving problems, so whether you are trying this out for the first time or whether you are an experienced professional designer, the same kind of processes have to be carried out.

Working from a design brief

A simple way of looking at the design process is set out below. It is called a Design Loop.

EFFICIENCY

Let us break down the stages of design as shown in the diagram. This should help you to understand why each stage is important and how, altogether, they will help you to achieve the most satisfactory result possible. It is important to make full notes as you work and to keep all your sketches and the results of your experimental work. Finally, put all the work in your design folder and take a photograph of the finished work so that you have it as a record of what you made.

Design loop

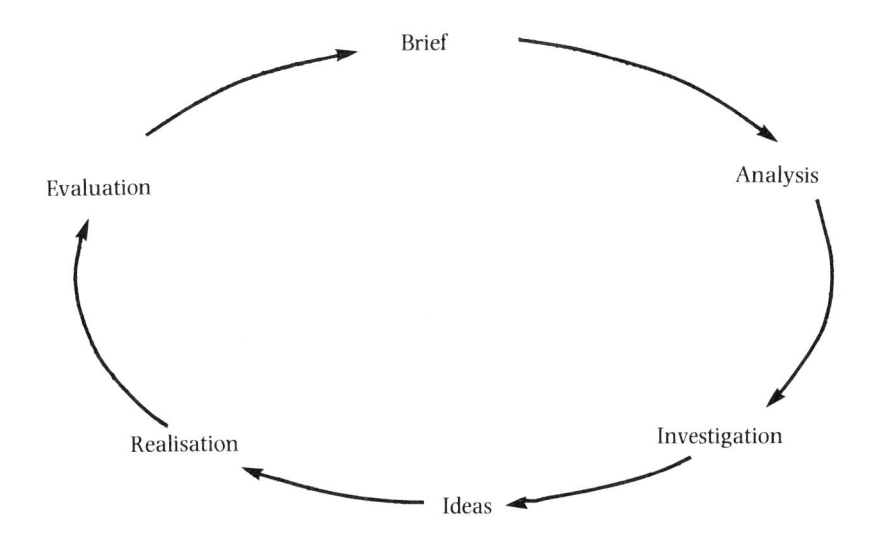

Brief → Analysis → Investigation → Ideas → Realisation → Evaluation → Brief

We start with a brief, which is a statement of what is required.
Brief: Design a cushion to be used in a location of your own choice. Use 'my favourite food' as the design source and make up the cushion using any suitable materials and techniques.

43

Stage 1 Analysis of brief   Ask yourself the following questions and as you collect information, keep it in your design file.

Cushions
- What are cushions?
- Where are they used?
- Why are they used?
- What do ready-made cushions look like?
- What do they cost to buy?

Room
- Where will my cushion be used?
- What is the colour scheme of the room?
- Will my cushion go on existing furniture?
- Will it be a floor cushion?

Foods
- What is my favourite food?
- Does it come in a packet, tin, wrapper?

Stage 2 Investigation   Ask yourself questions about design sources, types of fabric suitable, types of techniques possible, types of fillings and fastenings.

Design   Collect pictures, wrappers, packets, etc. and begin to make coloured sketches of them. Do not finally make up your mind which one you will choose just yet.

Fabrics   Look in the 'bit' box and collect samples of fabric which you feel will be right for your different types of food. For example: What would be best for an ice cream sundae? What would be the correct colour and texture?

Decoration   Could you dye or paint fabrics to add the detail? Would quilting, appliqué or stitchery help to achieve the desired effect? If so, try them out.

SAFETY

Types of filling   Have a look inside any cushions that you have at home, what types of fillings are used? How safe are they? Carry out some tests to find out.

EFFICIENCY

Fastening   How could my cushion cover be fastened? Look at cushions in the shops and at home and list the different methods of fastening you find in use. Would it be worthwhile putting in a zip? Which method would be cheapest? Find out the cost of different methods, e.g. velcro.

Stage 3 Ideas   This is the stage where you begin to try out some of your ideas. Sketch, using colours, the shapes that you feel would be successful. Begin to think about a possible solution. Ask yourself:
- As a result of my investigations, what seems to be the best solution to the problem set in the brief?
- Which food 'shape' will I use for my cushion?
- What colour will it be?
- How will I achieve the effects I want?
- How will I make a pattern for the cushion?

When you have answered all these questions and considered all the alternatives, then you will be able to make a final design decision based on your own good judgment.

Stage 4 Realisation This should be the most enjoyable part of the design process. You are now able to put into practice all your decisions. Your pattern will be made, fabric cut out, decorated and sewn together to make the cushion.

Make a cushion pad to go inside the cover to help it hold its shape.

Stage 5 Evaluation This is a very important stage.
Once you have finished making your cushion, you may feel that the work is complete. Actually, there is one more stage to go through.

Question: What does Evaluation mean?

Answer: It means putting your cushion to use and then looking at it critically after a period of time to see how well it is standing up to wear.

| AESTHETICS |
| EFFICIENCY |

Ask yourself the following questions:
How does the finished design compare with my original idea?
How well does it look in the room?
Is the cushion strong, are the seams splitting?
Does the decoration look good? Is it coming off?
Is the cushion still a good shape?
How much have I learned whilst designing and making up the cushion?
Can I identify which parts of the work I did well and which I did not do so well?
Could I have done it differently?
Could I improve on it? If so, how?
Am I pleased with the result?

As you can see, solving a design problem involves you in many different activities. Each time you tackle a new design brief, you will become more familiar with the method of working and, in time will become more efficient in the way that you work and organise your time.

Look again at the Design Loop on page 43 and you will see that you have completed the exercise but that 'Evaluation' points you back to the brief. This is because you must always judge your finished results against what you set out to achieve.

Now let us look at individual elements of design as applied to textiles.

COLOUR

AESTHETICS

Colour is one of the most important elements to consider when designing in textiles, or, as a consumer, buying a textile article.

It is important to learn how colour 'works', to appreciate that no colour is bad, and to learn to enjoy using colour and not be afraid of it.

Many people have fixed ideas about colour. We often hear people say 'I hate that colour' or 'I love that colour'. Strong feelings are expressed about colour but most of us do not really appreciate its value as a means of personal expression, to create atmosphere and mood, but above all to be enjoyed and used.

These days there are no hard and fast rules about which colours go together. You may have heard sweeping statements like 'blue and green should never be seen' and also familiar sayings like 'red for danger', 'yellow bellied' and so on. Colour likes and dislikes often stem from a combination of cultural influences, taboos, family influences and of course, our own instinctive feelings.

We may have been dressed in certain colours as young children, have disliked our school uniform or listened to superstitions, like 'green is unlucky'. All these factors may have had an influence on our choice of colour but it is important to have a sound knowledge of colour and the way it works.

KEY INVESTIGATION

Collect as many small (5 cm × 5 cm) samples of fabrics of different colours as you can. New fabric is not necessary, search the 'bit' box or cut up old clothes to obtain an interesting selection.

▷ ANALYSIS

Work in groups of 2 or 3 pupils.

1. Together, arrange the samples into colour 'families', i.e.,
    - warm colours,
    - cool colours,
    - neutrals,
    - brights,
    - pastels,
    - earthy colours,
    - jewel colours, and any other categories you can think of.

COLOUR

Mount the fabrics on pieces of card in their 'families'. Put them close together as solid areas rather like a simple patchwork using an adhesive like PVA.
2 Look at colour schemes currently used in textile goods in the shops.

EVALUATION

1 Taking each of the colour families from the investigation, pair each up with a situation where colour choice would be important, e.g. clothing for a walking holiday in the Lake District, colour choice: earthy with some brights.
   Give your reasons for each colour choice.
2 Which colours are currently 'fashionable' and why?

INVESTIGATION EXTENSION

Imagine that within your group, you are concerned with producing the new colour schemes for a collection of *either* fashion garments *or* household textiles.

1 Select approximately six or eight pictures of suitably fashionable articles from advertisements, catalogues or magazine articles.
2 Make tracings of these to obtain simple silhouette drawings or draw free-hand if you can.
3 Discuss the type of colour scheme that you feel would be relevant to those articles chosen. Transfer the shapes on to cartridge paper and use paint or any other suitable medium to colour in your drawings with your chosen 'colour family'.
4 Cut out the painted illustrations and mount these on a stiff piece of card or board together with samples of fabric and thread that help to extend the idea of your chosen 'colour family'.
5 Give your collection a suitable name. You will then have produced your own Colour Story Board or Trend Table. Some recent colour collections have been named 'Down Town', 'Sierra Nevada', and 'Rock Shock'.

Colour from natural dyes

ENVIRONMENT INTERACTION

In textiles colour can be built in at any stage of production, at the fibre, yarn, fabric or finishing stage. The colour that is used to colour textile products is called dye. Dyes have been used for centuries to colour fabrics but of course, some fibres have a natural colour that is desirable as it is, such as with Jacob sheep's wool which comes in shades from cream to grey and chocolate brown. Originally dyestuffs were made entirely from natural sources, from animal or plant material or minerals. Early man discovered the dyeing properties of these materials over a long period of time and they remained the only method of colouring textiles until well into the 19th century.

It is thought that the first colours applied to fabrics were in the form of stains from materials like brightly coloured berries and coloured earths, soot from fires and the juices from insects. These early colours would have faded quickly or washed off so it was found necessary to use some other substance to help stain the fabric permanently. These substances, known as mordants, were probably found by accident. They were generally salts, such as were found in sea water and urine. Mordant dyeing was practised by the ancient Egyptians.

> Pliny the Elder wrote in AD70:
> 'the white cloth being first stained in various places, not with dyestuffs, but with drugs, which have the property of absorbing colours. These applications do not appear on the cloth, but when the cloths are afterwards plunged into a cauldron containing the dye liquor they are withdrawn fully dyed of several colours, according to the different properties of the drugs which have been applied to different parts; nor can the colours be afterwards removed.'

EFFICIENCY

From the above description, we discover the secret of colour-fast dyeing. The fabric was first treated with a mordant, it was then immersed in a vat of dye, heated, and when rinsed out after the prescribed time, was 'colour fast', i.e. fast to light and washing.

The mordanting of fabric therefore plays a vital role in the dyeing process and it will be seen, that different mordants used with the same dyestuff will produce totally different colours.

KEY INVESTIGATION

Carry out a literature search and use other references available to find out the various substances that have been used as natural dye colour.

1. List the substances under headings thus:
   ANIMAL   to include insects, shellfish
   VEGETABLE   to include roots, stems, leaves and flowers
   MINERAL
2. Make a table like the one at the top of page 49 showing the various colours that could be obtained from these natural sources. Use the letters A, V, M to indicate origins.

DYEING EXPERIMENTS

	Red	Blue	Yellow	Green	Purple	Black	Origin
Cochineal beetle							A
Madder plant							V

The scouring and preparation section of a dye house in the 1920s

Dyeing experiments

Before you begin to dye, the raw materials must be prepared. Your teacher will provide you with some fleece or if this is unobtainable, some pure wool yarn in a natural colour.

The fleece will have to be washed in order to remove the dirt and grease before dyeing can take place. The yarn does not need to be washed. Rain water, melted snow, lake or stream water may be used but if none of these is available, use a water softener, vinegar or ammonia to soften hard tap water.

Stale human urine is one of the best cleaners and conditioners of wool but few of us would care to try it! In Scotland the Highland tweed-makers (of Harris Tweed) still use it as do dyers in other parts of the world.

Washing the Fleece

Method

1. Fill a bowl with hand-hot softened water.
2. Add liquid detergent (e.g. Stergene) at the rate of one capful to 6 litres of water.
3. Add the fleece (wool) and leave to soak for an hour.
4. Lift the wool out and drain it in a colander. Do not squeeze it.
5. Repeat the washing process once more.
6. Rinse the wool in tepid water until all traces of lather have disappeared.
7. Spread the wool out on an old sheet preferably outdoors on a blowy, sunny day.

NOTE: If the wool is to be mordanted at once, it may be used slightly damp but if it is to be stored, ensure that it is thoroughly dry.

Preparing mordants

SAFETY

Before using mordants and dyestuffs, some basic rules apply.
1 Never use the equipment used for dyeing for cooking afterwards. Old discarded saucepans, basins and bowls are ideal but ensure that they have no cracks or holes.
2 Stirring rods can be glass ones from a laboratory or you can improvise by using old wooden spoons or even garden canes.
3 Drying out of doors is preferable but indoor drying can be done on sheets of newspaper spread on the floor or on an old clothes airer.

HEALTH

4 It is very important to wear rubber gloves when handling mordants and dyes and when clearing up.
5 It is vital to keep a notebook of the recipe, time taken and sample produced.

The preparation of the wool by mordanting is important if you are to see a good result.

Mordants may be used as follows:
a on washed, damp wool, or
b in the dyebath, or
c before and after dyeing for extra colour fastness.

Many common substances may be used as mordants such as salt, vinegar, urine, wood ash, oak bark, copper filings. Dyes may be obtained from many of the wild and cultivated plants that are commonly seen in gardens, open spaces and the countryside. Try the following recipes and once you have an idea of how the dye colour is obtained, you can experiment with any likely material you have to hand.

Equipment for mordanting wool

DYEING EXPERIMENTS

Recipes for mordants

Dissolve the substances in enough boiling water to cover.

ALUM
4 teaspoons alum
1 teaspoon cream of tartar

IRON
2 teaspoons ferrous sulphate
1 teaspoon cream of tartar

COPPER
4 teaspoons copper sulphate crystals
2 teaspoons cream of tartar

CHROME
$\frac{1}{2}$ teaspoon bichromate of potash

General Instructions for Mordanting Wool

Method
1. Weigh the wool and allow 1 litre of water to every 28 g fleece or yarn.
2. Loosely tease out washed fleece or tie yarn into small hanks.
3. Pour the water into a suitably-sized saucepan and put on to heat until tepid.
4. Dissolve the mordant in enough boiling water to cover it then add it to the saucepan of tepid water.
5. Add the wool and simmer gently for half an hour.
   (Keep a lid on the saucepan when using bichromate of potash.)
6. Drain the wool and squeeze it gently.
7. *Always* use rubber gloves when working with mordants.

Preparing Dye Baths

Method
The following suggested plant material could be used but experiment with any others available locally or seasonally. Flowers may be difficult to obtain in the quantities required but good colours will result from using them. Leaves, fruits, roots, bark and skins may be easier to obtain.

A useful fact to remember is to use twice the weight of plant material to that of the fibre you wish to dye.

The plant material, particularly the woody bark, etc., needs to be soaked for some days before use, so prepare it in good time.

Equipment
saucepan
sieve

Flowers
Goldenrod
Pansies
Poppies
Dahlias
Marigolds

Pick the flowers when in full bloom, soak them for one hour in cold water. Simmer them gently in a saucepan for one hour then strain in a sieve and use liquor as a dye.

Leaves
Herbs
Cabbage—shredded
Forsythia (leaves)
Dock
Bracken

Soak the leaves in cold, soft water for two days.
Simmer them gently in a saucepan for one hour, strain and use liquor as a dye.

Fruits and roots
Elderberries
Carrots—cut up into slices
Beetroot—cut up into cubes
Blackberries
Acorns—cut in half

Soak the fruit or roots in cold water for one to two days depending on ripeness. Simmer gently for one hour in a saucepan, strain and use liquor as a dye.

Bark, skins and twigs
Walnut shells
Onion skins
Alder
Willow
Oak

Soak in cold water for two or three days depending on toughness, adding one tablespoon vinegar for very woody material. Simmer gently for one hour in a saucepan, strain and use liquor as a dye.

Using natural dyes

Once you have produced dye liquor, this is how to use it.
1   Put the strained dye liquor into a saucepan.
2   Add the mordanted wool.
3   Simmer gently for about one hour. Cool.
4   Remove wool carefully and rinse it in cold salted water.
5   Wash the wool with soap flakes, rinse thoroughly and dry it.

DYEING EXPERIMENTS

KEY INVESTIGATION

EFFICIENCY

1. Divide yourselves into four groups—A, B, C and D—each group preparing, in one mordant, 112 g of either fleece or wool yarn divided into four equal portions.
2. Identify the wools as shown below:
   Group A: alum mordant—tie each portion into one loose knot.
   Group B: iron mordant—tie each portion into two loose knots.
   Group C: copper mordant—tie each portion into three loose knots.
   Group D: chrome mordant—tie each portion into four loose knots.

   If you are using fleece, divide it into four portions and tag each with one, two, three or four pieces of string.
3. Mordant the skeins of wool following the instructions given on page 51.
4. Each group prepare one dye bath using any of four different plant materials available, i.e. four dye baths between all the groups.
5. Dye the mordanted wool following instructions given on page 52 putting each one of the four portions into different dyes.
   NOTE: Results will take some time to achieve as mordanting and dyeing take about one hour each.
6. Prepare a board on which to mount the dyed samples. Prepare labels.

ANALYSIS

1. What range of colours did the different dye stuffs yield?
2. What effects did the different mordants have on the colours?
3. Did any one colour predominate?
4. What effects, if any, did the mordants have on the feel of the wool or fleece samples?
5. Did the dyes stain the equipment used?

EVALUATION

1. Natural dyes generally give quite different colours from commercially produced ones. What do you consider to be the main differences?
2. Do you consider the time taken to produce colours from natural sources worthwhile?

53

INVESTIGATION EXTENSION

If there is a collection of old textiles in a museum or gallery near to your school or home, make a visit and look particularly at the colours used in old tapestries, embroideries, rugs or printed fabrics. Make colour notes and sketches of the articles, particularly noting the date and country of origin.

Modern dye stuffs

As already mentioned, natural dyes were used right up until the 19th century to colour fabrics and yarns. In the 1850s at the age of eighteen, William Henry Perkin, a student at the Royal College of Chemistry in London, discovered, by accident the first 'synthetic' dye. The colour he produced was the first aniline dye and commercially was called 'purple aniline'. Silk dyers in Lyon suggested the name 'mauve' for the colour and it became very fashionable. The English nicknamed it 'Perkins Purple' and it was quickly followed by other bright, strong colours—magenta, blue, violet and green. The effect on the public was stunning as fashionable ladies craved the new strong colours for their gowns and furnishings. These early synthetic dyes were rather unstable in that they faded quickly and many decades of research were needed before scientists came up with the idea of chemically combining the dye itself with the textile fibre. These dyes were called 'reactive' dyes. In 1955, ICI became the first company to put these cellulose, i.e. cotton, silk reactive dyes on the market. These are similar to the type of dyes that we can buy today, which are known as household dyes and made by ICI under the name Dylon. If you go into a store selling dye you will see a great range of colours, indeed it is now possible to buy small quantities of dye for all manner of household dyeing needs such as Wash 'n' Dye. Useful booklets are available which give us many different ideas for using the dyes to transform our homes and our clothing.

KEY INVESTIGATION

You will be provided with a small quantity of Dylon dye. Read the instructions carefully and dye a *cotton* item such as an old white T-shirt or shirt or pillowcase.

▷ **ANALYSIS**

Study the garment carefully after dyeing is complete.
1. Is the colour as expected?
2. Is the colour patchy?
3. Has the sewing thread used to make up the garment been dyed in the same way?
4. Have any of the garment's buttons changed colour?

□ **EVALUATION**

1. Find out how much the dye cost and estimate how many garments/articles could be dyed from one small container of dye.
2. Have the articles been improved in appearance?
3. If the results were not satisfactory, say why not.
4. Read the instructions again and state why you think it is important to follow them carefully.

INVESTIGATION EXTENSION

How could your own room at home be transformed by the use of dyes? Which colours would you use and why?

LET'S EXPERIMENT WITH DYES

Resist dyeing

In certain countries of the world, craftsmen and women down the ages have perfected methods of dyeing fabric which does not produce an all over even effect which is desirable when using modern household dyes.

Such methods are known as 'resist' dyeing and have been developed by using various means to stop the dye penetrating the complete piece of fabric. The 'resist' can be in the form of tightly knotted and tied fabric such as in tie and dye methods, or in the use of a greasy substance such as wax which is applied to certain areas of the fabric and is known as 'batik'. Both these methods are worth experimenting with as beautiful results can be obtained quite simply. Yarns may also be dyed by resist methods and then woven or knitted up into fabric.

DESIGN MATTERS

Fabrics on which resist dyeing methods have been used

KEY INVESTIGATION

Your teacher will provide you with books, leaflets or slides. Using the reference material available, make notes on the following resist methods. Tabulate your findings as shown.

1 Wax batik,
2 starch paste resist,
3 tie and dye: microwave dyeing,
4 tritik,
5 ikat,
6 spray dyeing.

Resist	Area or country of origin	Materials used	Equipment used	Use of fabrics
Wax batik	Indonesia	Hot wax, cotton fabric	tjanting or tjap	Sarongs, lengths of fabric wound around the body
Starch paste				
Tie and dye				
Tritik				
Ikat				
Spray dyeing				

RESIST DYEING

▷ **ANALYSIS**

1 What are the major differences between the different methods?
2 What kind of designs are produced by the different methods?
3 Does the country of origin have a bearing on either the methods or the type of designs produced?
   If so, why?

☐ **EVALUATION**

1 What makes these techniques unique?
2 Try working a sample of one or more of these techniques following the instructions given below.
   Evaluate your own results using these headings:
   a time taken,
   b degree of difficulty,
   c problems encountered,
   d ideas for future use.

NOTE: All new fabric for dyeing should be washed first to remove any dressing. For sample dyeing, fabric need only be 25 cm × 25 cm and pieces of old cotton sheets or pillowcases can be used.

Wax Batik

HEALTH

SAFETY

This can be dangerous and should only be done in small groups with the supervision of your teacher using the correct equipment. Wax must *never* be melted on a direct source of heat.

Equipment and Materials

EFFICIENCY

Wax pot—electric or improvised wax pot as shown or double saucepan
Tjanting (traditional Javanese tool)
Old bristle brush
Paraffin wax
Small piece beeswax
Cotton fabric pinned on to a frame or stretched on a board.
Cold water dye made up according to instructions.

Wax batik equipment

Method
1 Prepare a work area with newspaper to collect any drips of wax.
2 Heat the wax until it is melted and hot.
3 Put the tjanting and brushes into the wax to heat up. When the tools are removed from the hot wax, hold an old wooden spoon under them to prevent drips.
4 Experiment with the use of tjanting and brushes to make a series of lines and marks on the fabric using a simple design theme like 'water'. The wax will cool rapidly, so keep an eye on its temperature. It will not penetrate through the fabric and give a good resist if it goes cool.

5. When the waxing is complete, take the fabric off the frame or board and wet it thoroughly in cold water.
6. Place the fabric in a previously prepared bowl of *cold water dye* made up according to directions.
7. Leave fabric in for thirty minutes, then wearing rubber gloves, take it out, rinse it thoroughly and spread it out to dry on clean newspaper.
8. When completely dry, remove the wax by ironing it out between sheets of cheap, unprinted newsprint, remembering to replace wax-soaked paper as necessary.
9. The resist is now clear but you can go on to add more wax to the dried fabric, then dye it in another colour. Up to three dyes usually work well, after that the background colour can become murky.

Starch paste resist

This is a much safer method of obtaining similar results. The materials needed are readily available and easy to use.

EFFICIENCY

Equipment & Materials

Basin	Funnel
Wooden spoon	Flour—any type but wholemeal
Jug of water	Fabric pinned to a newspaper-
Squeezee bottle	covered board
or potter's slip trailer	Dye paint such as Dylon Colour Fun
Brush or sponge	

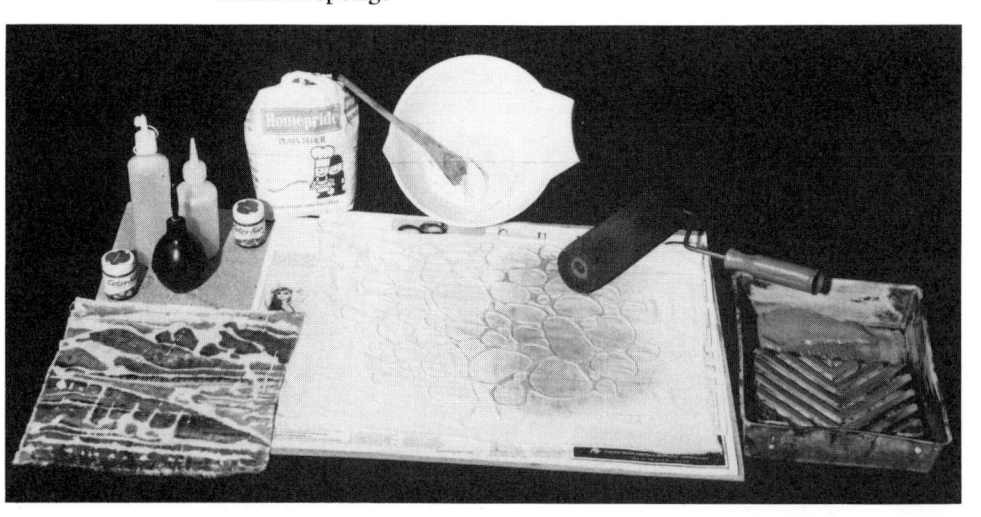

Starch paste resist equipment

Method
1. Put a quantity of flour into the basin and mix to a smooth paste with cold water (consistency of icing) with the wooden spoon.
2. Using the funnel half fill the squeezee bottle or slip trailer with paste.

3. Squeeze out a series of lines, spots, dashes and other simple marks on to the fabric. The paste should neither run nor be hard to force out of the nozzle. Adjust the consistency if necessary.
4. Leave the design to dry on a flat surface for 24 hours.
5. When dry, the paste will have shrunk and distorted the fabric. If you wish, you can gently crack the lines of paste but be careful not to peel them away completely.
6. Using dye paint, carefully brush or sponge the colour completely over the pasted surface.
7. When dry, peel off the paste with your fingers.
8. Set dye by ironing at correct temperature according to the instructions, then wash fabric gently to remove all traces of flour paste.

Tie and dye

Sometimes known as plangi, it is thought to be one of the oldest forms of patterning fabric and is also one of the simplest.

Equipment & Materials

EFFICIENCY

Scissors
Fine string or cotton thread (not sewing cotton) or raffia
Elastic bands
Cotton fabric (old sheets are excellent provided the fabric is not worn too thin)
Hot water or cold water dye made up according to instructions
Clothes pegs

Tie and dye equipment

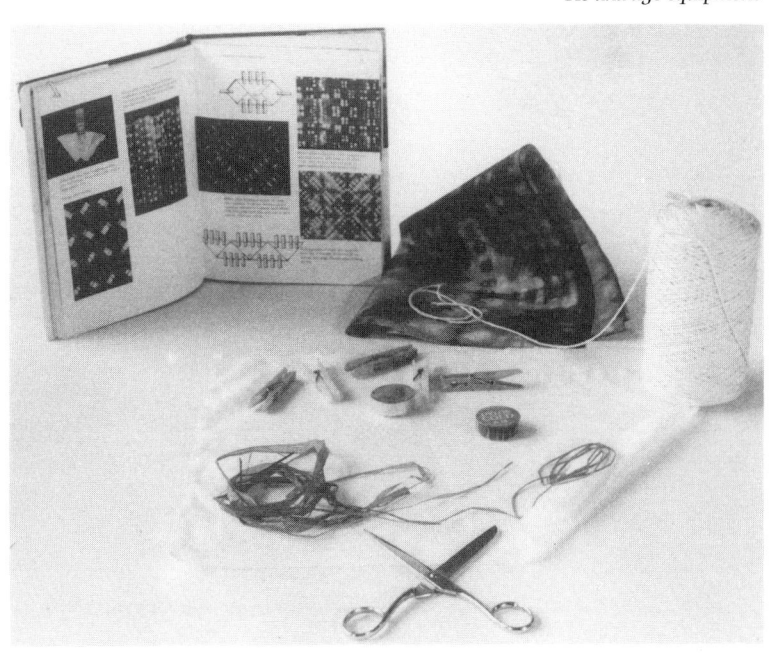

Method
1. Pull up the centre of your fabric sample with the fingers and gently stroke the fabric downwards.
2. Take an elastic band and put it over the fabric, binding it tightly in one place.
3. Repeat with more elastic bands or lengths of thread until the fabric is a tightly held bundle. Leave gaps of varying sizes between the areas of wrapping.
4. Wet the tied bundle in cold water, squeeze out surplus and place the sample into the dye, previously made up according to instructions.
5. Leave for 2–5 minutes in hot dye or half an hour in cold dye.
6. Remove the sample wearing rubber gloves and rinse it thoroughly under running water until no more loose dye comes out.
7. Unwrap the sample carefully and spread it out to dry.
8. If wanted, the process can be repeated, tying in different places to the first ties and putting the sample in another colour.
9. Try a similar sample but use clothes pegs to clip the fabric.

Tie and dye with a difference

Using natural fabric dye (Dylon) and cotton fabric, experiment with scrunching up the fabric, knotting, twisting and pleating. Prepare dye according to instructions in a plastic bowl, and wet the fabric squeezing out the surplus water. Then follow this method:
1. Put the fabric in the bowl of prepared dye.
2. Cover the bowl with a plastic bag or cling film.
3. Put bowl in microwave oven for four minutes on 'high'.
4. Remove bowl from oven.
5. Tip away dye and rinse fabric in cold water.
6. When water is running clear, untie knots, etc., and wash fabric in hot soapy water to remove remaining dye.
7. Dry away from direct heat and sunlight.

Tritik

This is a similar process to tie and dye but involves the use of a needle and thread.

| EFFICIENCY |

Equipment & Materials
Long, sharp needle
Pins
Strong sewing cotton
Soft cotton fabric
Hot or cold water dye made up according to instructions

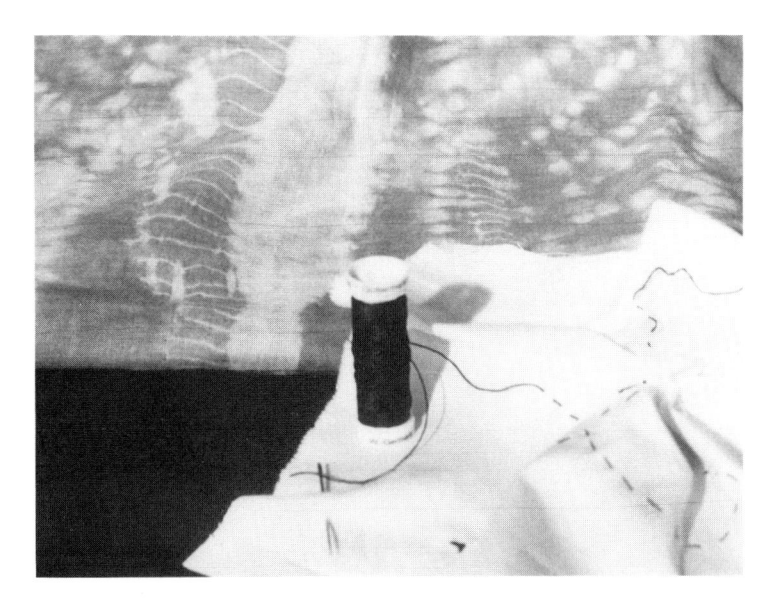

RESIST DYEING

Tritik

Method
1. Thread the needle and tie a strong knot in the end of the thread.
2. Sew wavy lines approximately 1 cm apart across the fabric using a long running stitch, when at the end of the line pull the thread from the needle and leave it hanging free.
3. When all desired lines are sewn in, pull the threads up very tightly one at a time and fasten the long ends by wrapping them around pins.
4. Wet the fabric in cold water and squeeze out the surplus.
5. Put the sample into the dye and leave for 2–5 minutes in hot dye, half an hour in cold dye.
6. When dyeing is complete, take out the sample and rinse it carefully under cold running water until no more loose dye comes out.
7. Take out the pins, and gently pull out the threads from the knotted end.
8. Hang up the sample to dry.

Ikat

A method of resist dyeing yarns before weaving or knitting.

Equipment & Materials

|EFFICIENCY|

A continuous length of cotton yarn such as dishcloth cotton folded by being wrapped around a piece of board or over the back of a chair.
Thread or raffia
Scissors
Card loom or knitting needles
Hot or cold water dyes made up according to instructions

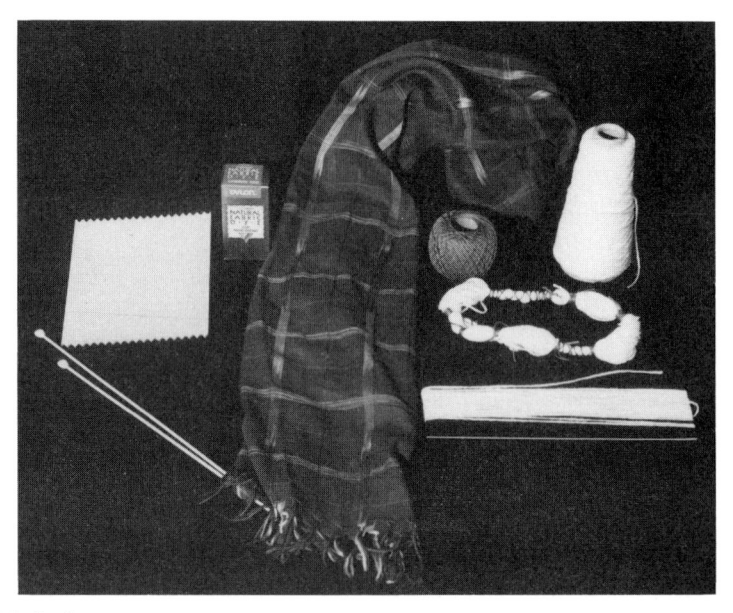

Ikat equipment

Method
1. Slide the yarn off the board or chair back and carefully lay it out on the table.
2. Taking small bundles of it at a time, wrap a section here and there by tightly tying thread around it at intervals of about 2 cm.
3. Carry on tying until the yarn is tied up in tight sections at regular intervals.
4. Place the wrapped strands into the dye and leave for 5–10 minutes in hot dye or half an hour in cold dye.
5. Take yarn out of dye and rinse it thoroughly under running water until all loose dye has come out.
6. Squeeze the yarn and blot it on kitchen paper.
7. Hang the yarn up in a warm place to dry.
8. Untie the thread ties and shake out the yarn, wind it into a small ball.
9. Alternatively, you can dry the yarn, untie some areas, re-tie others and put it into a second colour.
10. Use the dyed yarn either as the warp on your card loom and weave a small piece of fabric using a plain coloured weft thread or knit a small stocking stitch sample on suitably-sized knitting needles.

Spray Dyeing

Liquid dye can easily be sprayed on to the fabric's surface and to achieve interesting results, the use of newspaper as a form of 'resist' is suggested. Of course, dyes may be sprayed directly on to fabrics without the newspaper resist, giving lovely soft effects of colour. A piece of fabric crumpled up and sprayed gives very interesting results.

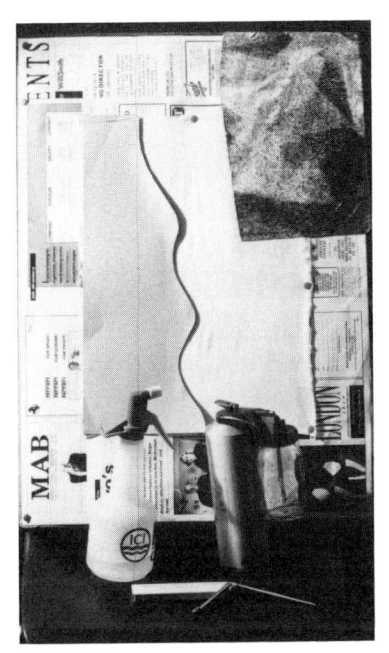

RESIST DYEING

Spray dyeing is easy to do but does require practice. The effect required is one of lightness and delicacy and this is achieved through blowing the dye on to the fabric in tiny spots of colour. Strictly speaking, this is not a true dyeing method because the fabric is not immersed in a dye bath, but it has been included because of the particularly pleasant results it gives using cold, liquid dye.

The use of the different spray methods will give slightly different results. In school, it may be possible only to use improvised tools but these will give good results with practice.

It must be remembered that all spray dyeing must be done on a vertical surface. You will not be able to control the work if you try to do this on a flat table surface.

If you have pin board or display boards around the room, these may be covered with newspaper to protect them from the dye. An improvised spray dyeing area can be produced by putting a chair on a table and leaning a board against it, making sure that *all* surfaces are covered with newspaper to protect them.

The fabric should be pinned to the board at a comfortable height depending on the spray method used.

Spray dyeing equipment

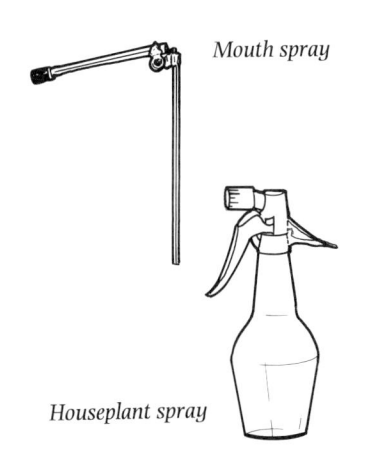

Mouth spray

Houseplant spray

Compressed air spray

EFFICIENCY

Equipment and Materials

Mouth spray or diffuser
  or houseplant spray
  or compressed air spray

Fabric
Cold dye made up according
  to instructions

Method
1. Cover the dyeing area with newspaper for protection.
2. Pin fabric to prepared vertical surface.
3. Pin newspaper strips to fabric in an interesting arrangement.
4. Fill container with dye.
5. Spray dye gently over fabric using backwards and forwards movement. Do not allow the tiny spots of colour to join up and cause the dye to run.
6. Remove the newspaper strips to reveal the resist pattern produced.
7. Re-pin strips on to different parts of the fabric and re-spray over using a different coloured dye.

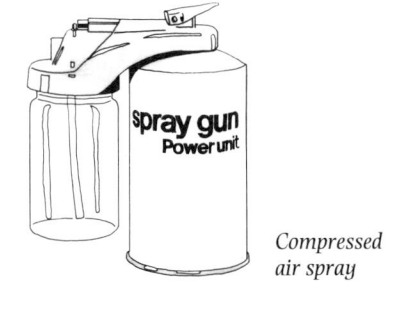

LET'S LOOK AT FABRIC PRINTING

As has been seen, colour dyeing of fabric involves a liquid dye and generally, immersion of the fabric or yarn in the dye bath. The dye penetrates the fibres of the fabric and the fabric will look much the same on the back as on the front.

By contrast, printed fabric uses a thickened dye in paste form and is put on selected areas of the fabric and appears on one side of the fabric only.

DESIGN MATTERS

Block printing

ENVIRONMENT INTERACTION

The earliest forms of printed fabric were made by block printing from hand carved blocks of wood. Earliest known examples date from the 5th to 6th century in Egypt but patterned garments, presumed to be printed, are to be seen in wall paintings of 2500 BC in China and India.

Wood block printing involves many different skills and continued until the use of metal engraved blocks in the 18th century and engraved roller printing in the 19th century. Blocks of hard wood, cut across the grain, were deeply carved into rich patterns using chisels and knives.

The method of printing wood blocks is simple. Rather like having your book stamped at the library, the uncut surface of the block is coated with dye and is then pressed firmly on to the fabric in the required place. Additional blocks carrying other colours could then be printed on top of the first colour. You may have experimented with potato cuts in your junior school or even produced lino prints. The principle is the same for all these methods, only the material for the block varies.

Block printing

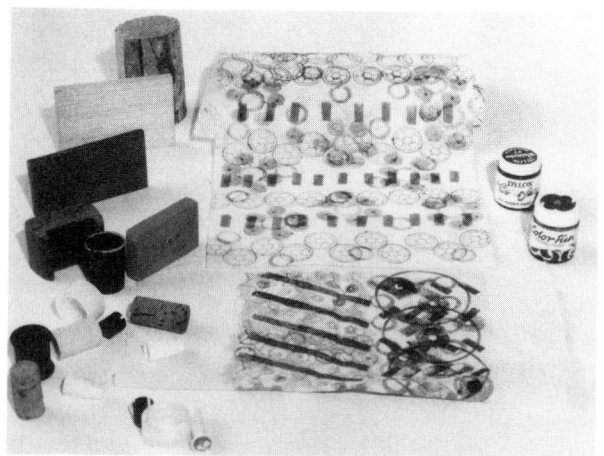

BLOCK PRINTING

KEY INVESTIGATION

EFFICIENCY

1. Make a collection of a number of objects that could be used as simple blocks. To start you off, here are a few suggestions:
   corks,   cardboard tubes,
   polystyrene scraps, offcuts of wood,
   cotton reels,   plastic bottle caps.
2. Take a piece of old sheeting and stick it down to a pad of newspaper using masking tape. If there is a fabric printing table available use that, of course.
3. Make a printing pad as shown to hold the dye.

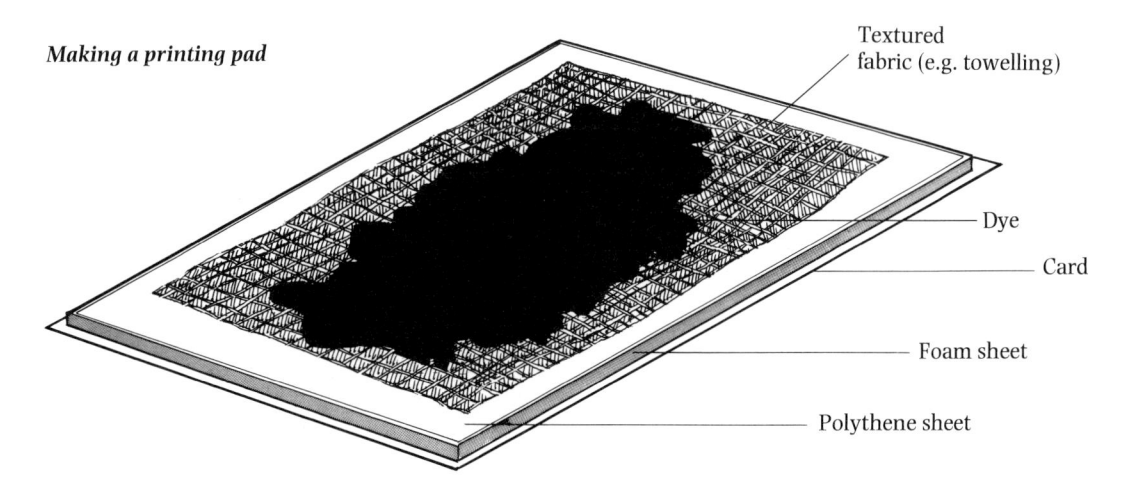

Making a printing pad

Labels: Textured fabric (e.g. towelling), Dye, Card, Foam sheet, Polythene sheet

1. Take a piece of stiff card or plyboard.
2. Cut out a piece of foam sheet to cover.
3. Cover the foam sheer with polythene and tape to the back of the board.
4. The printing pad can be washed and re-used.

4. Dye paint (Dylon Colour Fun) or any available dye paste slightly diluted should now be brushed on to the pad and allowed to soak well in.
5. Taking one of the 'blocks' at a time, press it into the dye and print it on the fabric, noting the kind of mark it leaves behind.
6. Build up small patches of each print so that you can identify one from the other. Do not just dot the prints around at random.
7. When dry, fix the dye according to the manufacturer's instructions.

▷ ANALYSIS

1. Which 'blocks' gave the most satisfactory results? Which the least?
   Make a table to record your results.
2. Which 'blocks' would you consider using again and in what way?
3. How could you control the print better?

☐ EVALUATION

From the results of your investigations with simple block prints, what do you consider to be the advantages and disadvantages of this technique?

Produce a poster, decorated with block prints, which could be put up in the textiles room to help others enjoy practising this craft.

INVESTIGATION EXTENSION

Carry out the following design brief:

Using two or three of your blocks and more than one colour, design and print a richly decorative border pattern that could be used for a specific purpose, such as table mats or a child's pinafore.

Stencil printing

In contrast to block printing which involved carving wood or engraving metal, stencil printing is relatively easy to do as it involves cutting the design out of thick waxed paper and pushing the dye through the holes to the fabric underneath. We have probably all played with stencils as children, creating pictures of animals or flowers and no doubt have all found plastic stencils useful for lettering. For stencil-printed textiles the principle is much the same.

The earliest stencils were produced by the Japanese in the 8th century and although the technique is simple, they achieved a very high standard of fine detail and intricacy of pattern with their stencil prints on silk and cotton.

In recent years stencil printing has been revived as a form of interior decoration and there are many kits on sale which include the cut stencils, special brushes and instructions for printing repeat patterns on furniture and walls. This particular form of stencilling originated in America in the 19th century and, although strictly speaking not of interest here, the designs that were produced would work equally well on fabric.

STENCIL PRINTING

Stencil printing

KEY INVESTIGATION

Using references provided, make notes and sketches on the designs and techniques which have been used for stencil printing.

ANALYSIS

1. What tools and materials are used to carry out stencil printing?
2. What type of designs make the most successful stencil prints?
3. What do the designs have in common?
4. What points of safety must be observed when cutting stencils?
5. What other form of fabric printing is similar to stencil printing?

EVALUATION

Having carried out this investigation, you should have enough information to be able to try some stencil printing of your own.

Design a simple motif and cut it as a stencil. Print it using available equipment and materials.

Keep all your experiments and mount them in your folder adding full notes on each stage of the work.

INVESTIGATION EXTENSION

1. Design and cut a stencil to fill a 12 cm square using a motif based on a tile pattern.
2. Using dye paste applied with a stencil brush, sponge, or paint roller, experiment with as many ways of printing the design in a block of four as you can. Some suggestions are shown overleaf.

67

DESIGN MATTERS

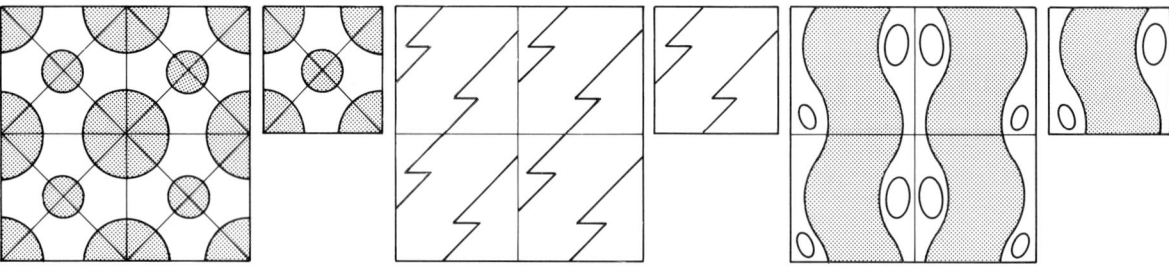

3 Select one of your ideas and print it using dye paint or similar on fabric for a cushion or chair seat cover. Fix the dye according to instructions and make up the article.

Recent developments in dye products

Transfer dyes

Liquid dyes and dye pastes have been in use for many years. The most recent development in fabric printing has been the invention, in the 1970s, of the transfer dye process.

EFFICIENCY

This came about in answer to the need to find a dye suitable for use on the new synthetic (man-made) fibres. Traditional dyes were found to be unstable on polyester fabrics and experiments produced an entirely new concept in fabric printing. In all previous printing methods, the dye had to be printed one colour at a time such as you would have used to produce your sample fabrics. The new process of

Transfer printing equipment

transfer printing has enabled all the colours in a design to be printed in one operation. First the dye is actually printed on paper, then fabric and paper are together passed through rollers and heat and pressure applied. During this process, the dye is transferred from the paper to the fabric. The waste product of this new industry is often re-cycled—you have probably all bought flowers wrapped in patterned paper, this is what the paper looks like after it has transferred its colour to fabric.

Although liquid transfer dyes are available these are quite expensive but it is possible to buy quite cheaply, transfer wax crayons.

Paper recycled from the transfer dye process

1. Using transfer wax crayons, experiment on newsprint paper with a number of different lines, textures and patterns. Try overlapping colours, pressing hard or gently and finding as many ways as you can of exploring their potential.
2. Place samples of three different white fabrics, pure cotton, polyester, polyester/cotton, on an old ironing sheet. Cut your crayoned sheet into three strips and place one face downwards on each fabric.
3. Cover *all* samples with a thin sheet of paper.
4. Heat up iron to medium temperature.
5. Press the iron down hard on the samples leaving it in place for a few moments.
6. Take away the iron, remove the paper and the cut strips to reveal the prints.

ANALYSIS

1. Which fabric gave the best results? Which the least?
2. Look at the colour differences between the crayons themselves, the drawing and the fabric print. Make a note of these.
3. What happened to overlapping colours?
4. What was the effect of putting light or hard pressure on the crayons as you used them?
5. Check to see if the colours have changed by the next day.

EVALUATION

Transfer printing should be easy, safe and effective.
1. How could you ensure good results every time?
2. Do you think the iron temperature is important? If so, why?
3. What kinds of design would give the best results in transfer printing?

INVESTIGATION EXTENSION

Collect some samples of florists' wrapping paper. Cut out simple shapes from these and place them face down on to polyester/cotton fabric. Cover them with a sheet of clean scrap paper and press down firmly with a hot iron to transfer the design.

Experiment with a combination of transfer paper and transfer crayons.

Dye Pens and Crayons

Craft dye may also be purchased in a form looking rather like a felt pen and in crayon form. These products are expensive and may not be available to you in school but it is worth knowing about them. Usually they are sold in packs of ten or twelve giving one of each colour.

EFFICIENCY

The dye 'pens' are very useful for putting in detail but are far too expensive to use on a large area. They can be used directly on fabric and should be fixed by being ironed with a hot iron when they are thoroughly dry.

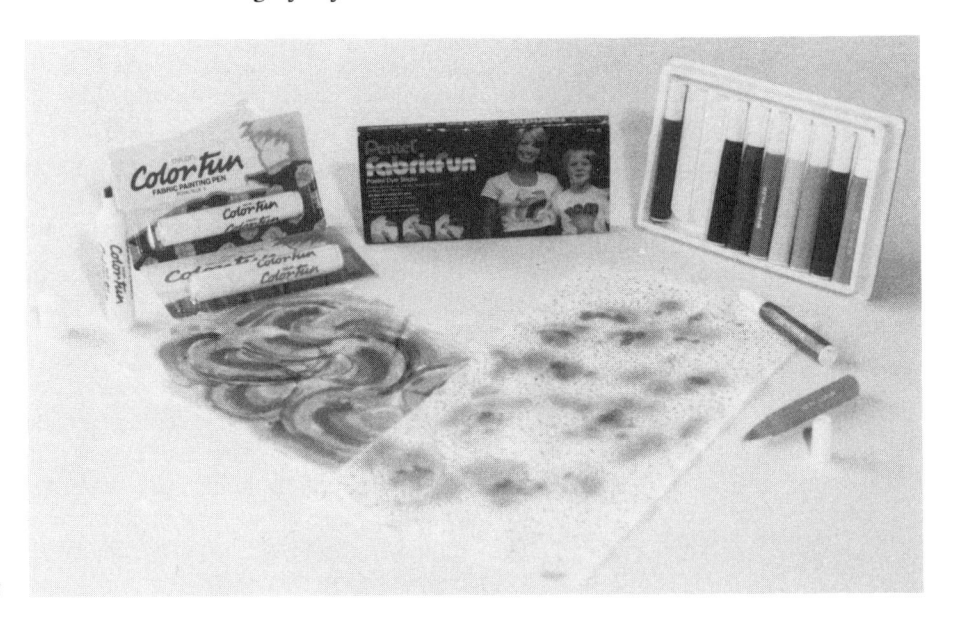

Dye pens and crayons

The dye crayons are easy to use though they can be messy. They are like very soft oil pastels and can break easily. Like the dye pens, they are used directly on the fabric's surface.

With both of these new types of dye it is advisable, if you are using them, to pin out the fabric firmly on to a board. A light touch is essential to give good results.

The colours are bright and strong and work well with other methods of dyeing and printing, adding detail, and allowing you to 'draw' into the design.

Combinations: printing and dyeing with other techniques

The techniques described are all basically simple to do and require the minimum of specialist equipment. If you have had a chance to try them all, then you will begin to recognise the individual characteristics of each. However, sometimes it is a good idea to use the dyed or printed fabric as a background for other techniques, this is often a good way to 'rescue' a rather disappointing piece of work.

| AESTHETICS |

The following suggestions could be tried but do experiment as much as possible. Sometimes remarkable effects can be achieved by working with two or three different techniques on one piece of work. These mixed media designs are often rich in colour, texture and pattern and are very enjoyable to do.

1. Freely paint liquid dye or dye paste on to wet or dry fabric. Try using brushes of different sizes, old toothbrushes, sponges or scraps of rag or paper towel.
2. On resist dyed fabric try adding:
   free machine embroidery,
   hand stitchery,
   or use for patchwork.
3. Block and stencil prints look particularly good if hand stitchery or machine satin stitch is added.
4. Transfer printing is excellent combined with tie and dye.
5. Dye pens and crayons could be used to highlight any printed or dyed fabric.

As you will have seen, printing or dyeing your own designs need not be difficult.

Combination of dye with embroidery

> Dyes may be used to change the colour of fabrics and threads in many different ways and if instructions are followed carefully, there should be no problems. Surprising results often occur, you will learn to enjoy and understand colour in a more interesting way if you experiment with dyes, probably more than in any other way.

LET'S LOOK AT TEXTURE

In Section 2 when we were looking at methods of fabric construction, you would have been aware that the fibre, yarn and method of making the fabric will all have influenced its final appearance. Texture is a vital element in the study of textiles, since it is concerned with the surface and the 'feel' of the fabric.

| HUMAN DEVELOPMENT |

When very young children are in the process of learning about the world they live in, you notice that they reach out to grasp objects, they put them into their mouths and they play with them in their hands and toes. In fact, the whole of the baby's body is sensitive to

SAFETY

VALUES

the touch of materials. They develop their sense of 'touch' from these early times. Babies are wrapped in textiles from birth and are surrounded by the warmth, softness and comfort of textile products all their young lives. As children grow up, their need to touch can get them into trouble. Of course, for safety reasons it would be wrong to let them touch everything, but constantly being told 'not to touch' does eventually make children unsure or even afraid to touch as much as instinct tells them to.

When dealing with textiles, it is very important to develop our 'tactile' sense. Fabrics and threads cannot be fully understood and appreciated unless the senses of sight and touch are employed together.

If you go shopping for clothes or a length of material, it would be ridiculous to expect to know whether it was suitable for its purpose without first feeling it. Some fabrics have a much more interesting surface texture than others, some may not appeal at all. Many people find there are fabrics which they dislike just because of their texture. For instance, you either love or loathe velvet! When fabric has a plain colour, its surface appearance becomes very important. When a fabric is printed with a complex design then the actual surface texture may not be of so much significance.

KEY INVESTIGATION

1. Your teacher will provide you with a number of samples of fabric. Ignoring the colour, place them in categories according to their surface texture. Define your own categories but some suggestions might be:
   shiny, hairy, knobbly.
2. Mount the samples and write as full a description of each as possible.
3. Unravel a few threads from each sample and mount these alongside.

▷ ANALYSIS

1. Taking each sample in turn, say what you think caused its particular surface texture, fibre, yarn, construction or combination of these.
2. Take each sample in turn and describe its light-reflecting or light-absorbing qualities.
3. Take each sample in turn and describe its weight, thickness and density.

▲ Block printing experiment by 12-year-old pupil (see page 64)

◀ Sample of tie and dye for a turban cloth from Rajisthan, NW India (see page 59)

▲ Ikat—showing detail from large Indonesian wall hanging (warp-painted) (see page 61)

▲ Starch paste resist method used by a pupil aged 16 (see page 58)

Close-up of experimental piece of tapestry weave by 11-year-old pupil (see page 29) ▶

◀ *Rubbings from autumn leaves done as a transfer print using fabric crayons (see page 68)*

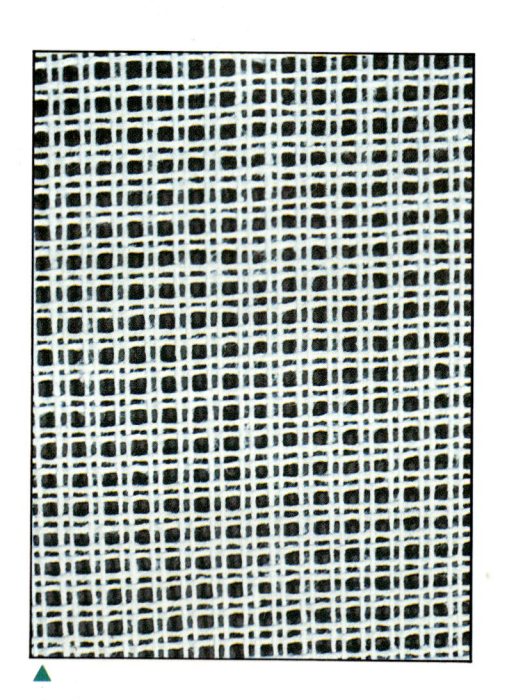

Variety of fabric textures (see page 71)

EVALUATION

1. In clothing why do you think the texture of a fabric is important particularly for the:
   - *a* overweight adult,
   - *b* underweight adult,
   - *c* baby,
   - *d* growing child,
   - *e* teenager?
2. In household textiles, what is particularly significant about texture of the choice of material for:
   - *a* carpets,
   - *b* bed linen,
   - *c* towels,
   - *d* tea towels,
   - *e* chair covers?

Let's create texture: surface stitchery

AESTHETICS

If you carried out any of the earlier exercises in knit and weave, then you would have been creating textural surfaces already. There are many interesting ways of building up surface interest.

One of the most versatile methods is to add stitches. This form of surface decoration has its origins in the distant past. Ever since man found a way of holding two or more animal skins together by means of a primitive needle and leather thong, decorative stitches have been practised. The simple straight stitch is the 'ancestor' of all the stitches that we use today from complicated knot stitches to the delicate embroidery produced by today's computerised sewing machines.

In the past, adding decorative stitches to garments signified status, particularly when the threads used were of precious metals and the spangles of semi-precious stones. You will know that the splendid garments of the past were seen to denote rank and position in society. Some of the most complex, rich and beautiful work of this kind was done in England in the Middle Ages but each country has its own traditions which developed in a similar way. The materials used were generally, like the dye stuffs, of local origin such as the fine silk embroideries of China when the art of 'sericulture', the production of silk was invented. In Europe, the materials used were wool and linen, in India cotton, in Egypt flax. Trade in these commodities developed and ideas for their use and decoration in complex stitches and designs were exchanged.

ENVIRONMENT INTERACTION

Embroidery, as it became known has been a means of adding rich, surface interest to fine fabrics for many centuries but was only carried out on the clothing and household textiles of the wealthy.

In the 19th century, embroidery became the hobby of the middle-class lady of leisure and was taught to all the young girls of the

DESIGN MATTERS

ENVIRONMENT INTERACTION

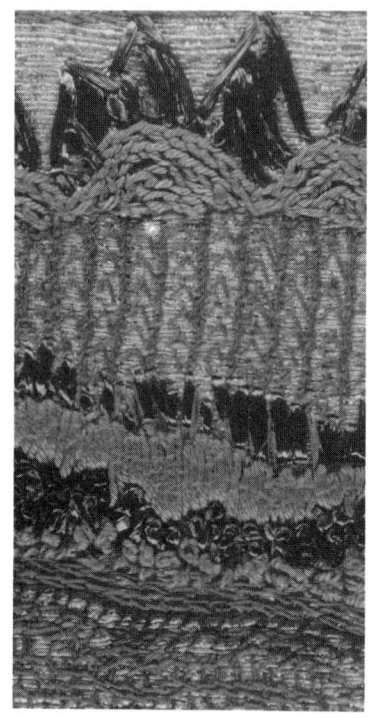

Stitch textures in design based on landscape

EFFICIENCY

household. Interestingly, all the great embroideries of the distant past were designed and worked by men as were most of the textile crafts.

The tradition of embroidery largely died out as a result of the two world wars 1914–18, 1939–45. Materials were scarce and a woman's role was beginning to change dramatically. Women were going out to work in great numbers, experiencing a life outside the home and enjoying a fuller life. Nevertheless the craft did not die out completely and has enjoyed a dramatic revival since the 1950s. Today there are more men and women enjoying the old craft of 'embroidery' than ever before.

Modern stitchery (for that is a better word to use) relies on a sound knowledge of design and techniques, uses a vast range of materials but above all, relies on the ability of the individual to try to express his/her own ideas. It is one of the most versatile textile crafts there is and can be done by people of either sex, any age or any ability.

Stitches, as already mentioned, are based on a simple straight line sewn into the fabric. The following investigation will help you to see something of the enormous potential of the craft.

KEY INVESTIGATION

Your teacher will put out a selection of different threads and also some more unconventional ones like knitting wools and weaving yarns. You may make your own 'threads' from torn strips of fabric, bits of string and leather thongs, cut up plastic bags and even strips of paper. You will also need a large-eyed needle and a piece of hessian, approximately 20 cm × 20 cm.

1. Select a range of different threads from thick to thin, rough to smooth but restrict yourself to a limited colour range.
2. Taking each thread or yarn in turn, thread your needle and make a series of short straight stitches close together, in patches on your hessian. The groups of simple stitches should be arranged in vertical, horizontal or diagonal patches.

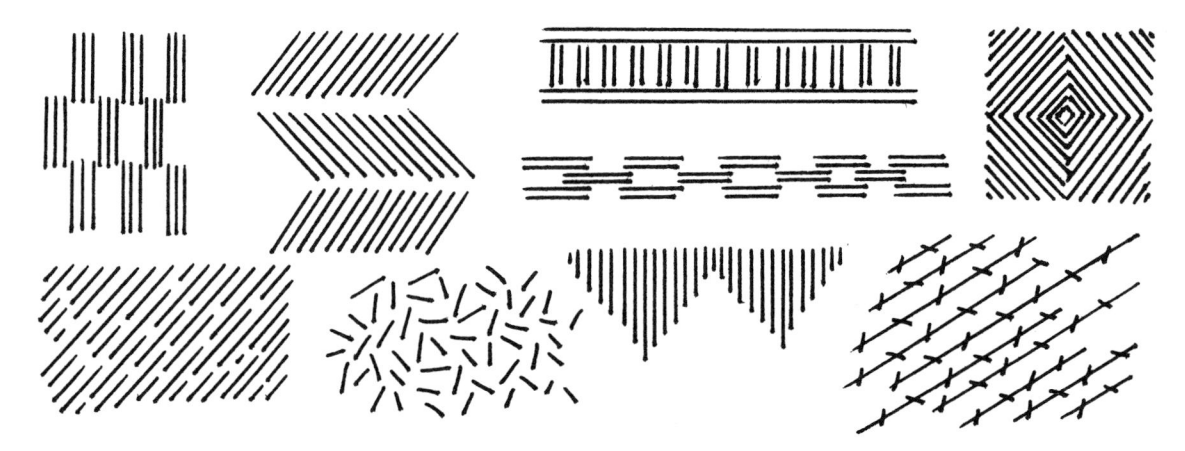

ANALYSIS

1. Stick a sample length of each thread you used into your notebook and describe the kind of stitch it made.
2. Comment on how easy or difficult it was to work with.
3. Comment on the textural differences of the different stitches produced, particularly where they were used close together.

EVALUATION

From the results of your investigation experiments, you should be able to put the information to use in this simple design brief.

Using your knowledge of threads and simple stitches design and work in suitable colours a small panel approximately 10 cm × 15 cm, based on an idea from one of the following:
  brickwork,
  rocks,
  water.
Use mainly simple, straight stitches but include variations such as overlapping. Couching may be used too. Complete your work by mounting it in a card mount.

INVESTIGATION EXTENSION

1. Design a canvas work-container for holding your small sewing equipment (scissors, tape, needles, etc.). Use different stitches to create an interesting surface texture. Use colours of your choice.
2. Design a small picture suitable for a young child to hang in his/her bedroom. Use mainly cross-stitch and some other counted thread embroidery to complete your design. Work on an evenweave fabric.
   NOTE: The following two design briefs could be worked in groups.
3. [VALUES] You have been asked to design and work a wall-hanging to be displayed in the entrance of a school for the blind and partially sighted. Your design should emphasise the tactile qualities of the materials and thread used.
4. [AESTHETICS] Design a set of four small pictures depicting a tree or trees during each of the four seasons. Be as imaginative as possible in your choice of materials and threads so that the tree/trees will have good textural qualities as well as showing appropriate colours.

Development of more complex stitches

What you have been doing is exploring the nature and versatility of the simplest stitch. If you look through any of the books on embroidery that are available in the textile room or school library, you will be amazed at how many different stitches there are. If you look at the pictures of stitches closely, you will see how varied they are; some are spiky, some rounded, some knotty, some loopy, some like dotted lines. Stitches also have interesting names, some are named after the places where they originated like Cretan, French knot, Pekinese and Roumanian couching. Others are named after their actual appearance, for example, feather, herring bone, chain and seeding.

EFFICIENCY

Some stitches are easy to do, some more difficult but it is always worth trying to learn a few new ones. These, once mastered, will give you a whole new range of effects. Sometimes the diagrams in the books which show you how to work the stitches are not very good so do not give up too easily. Ask your teacher for help.

Because there are so many stitches, it is tempting to think that a good piece of work should have many stitches included in it. This is not so. In fact it is better to restrict the number of different stitches used in one piece of work and perhaps use between two and four, but work many variations of these.

As you would have seen if you carried out the earlier investigation using straight stitch only, there were many ways of changing its appearance. These changes of size, direction, density or changes in the type of thread used are possible with any stitch. Look at a piece of embroidery from the past, either in a picture or an actual piece if you are near a museum which has such things on show. You will notice that the surface will be very rich and thickly decorated but the number of stitches probably restricted. Notice also how the person doing the work has made the stitches take up the shapes of the design.

KEY INVESTIGATION

1. Look at the photograph of this piece of embroidery from the 16th century (or if you like, select one of your own from references available).
2. Make a note of all the different stitches that were used. Look them up if you do not know their names.
3. Look at each stitch in turn and note in how many different ways they have been used. Make little sketches to illustrate these variations.

MORE COMPLEX STITCHES

▷ **ANALYSIS**

For each of the stitches you have discovered in the piece of antique embroidery you have studied decide what their main uses have been. Put your results in a table as below.

Name of stitch	Effect	Sketch
Chain stitch	1 outlining 2 filling in	

☐ **EVALUATION**

1 Write a short paragraph which describes typical domestic embroidery of the 16th century.
2 List the points which you feel could help you improve your own design and working of stitches.

INVESTIGATION EXTENSION

Design and work a small piece of stitchery approximately 12 cm × 20 cm which uses *three* different stitches only. Each of the three stitches must be used in more than one way, e.g. for outlines, or for filling spaces.

Base your design on *either*
a a cat curled up on a cushion
   or
b a building that you know well (it could be your own house).

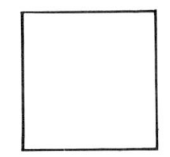

LET'S LOOK AT SHAPE AND FORM

Two-dimensional square

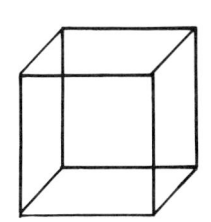

Three-dimensional cube

Firstly, what is the difference between shape and form, or do they mean the same thing? To a designer, shape generally refers to something that is two-dimensional, but form to something that is three-dimensional. So a flat picture has shape and a piece of pottery has form.

Everything that we see around us has shape or form. Our houses, schools, factories, hospitals and shops are all large buildings of different shapes, forms and sizes. Inside each, furniture, books, equipment and machinery are made from a variety of materials in countless different shapes and forms. It can be said that shape/form and the materials used to make it, are dependent on function. Function is the task that the object has to perform, so that we could look at the buildings we call homes and see that the concrete, glass, brick and metal 'box' that has been built is there to perform a function. In the case of our houses, it is to provide a building where a group of people can live, one that is safe to be in, comfortable, attractive and where we can eat, sleep, work, play, either together as a family or on our own or with friends.

ENVIRONMENT INTERACTION

The design of the shape/form of buildings such as we live in has evolved over many centuries. It is interesting to look up in the library the design of houses from the distant and more recent past and of the present day. As people's needs changed, skills developed and technological and economic changes took place, so the shapes of buildings changed too.

In clothing, similar needs have shaped the garments we wear. The history of costume is a fascinating study and worth looking into. Even as we look at the way modern clothes have evolved, we can see patterns emerging. Sometimes ideas from the past come back into fashion again: colours, shapes, styles in clothing today probably all have their origins to a certain extent in past fashions. We have looked briefly at clothing design in Section I but now need to discover exactly how the design is produced from an original idea to a finished garment in the shop.

HUMAN DEVELOPMENT

VALUES

We have been looking at shape related to man-made objects but of course, natural objects have shape and form too. Our own bodies are complex forms which change considerably from the time we are born to our old age. In your own class or year at school, there will be a tremendous variety of sizes and shapes. The clothing we wear has to change as our bodies change in size and shape but also in line with the changes in our age and interests or family, social and economic needs. Some people are unfortunate in that they have, through illness or at birth, not developed normally. Physically handicapped

HEALTH

people and those who have suffered a crippling disease like arthritis often have problems with joints and limbs in particular.

The clothing industry

Most of us buy our clothes ready-made from the shops or from mail order firms, very few people actually make their own clothes and even fewer use a dressmaker or tailor. If you have ever made a garment for yourself or for someone else, you will appreciate the links between the flat, two-dimensional pieces of fabric that you cut out, and the final finished three-dimensional garment.

The clothes which we buy ready-made are the products of the clothing industry. The industry is vast and is now an international one. Look at the labels inside some of your clothes and see where they were made.

Many people are employed in the clothing industry and they have different roles to play in the production of our clothes. Let us see how a garment is developed from the original designer's ideas to the familiar rails of garments which are displayed in our local shops.

The flow chart shows what a complex organisation the clothing industry is, but first, let's look at the role of fashion designers. The styles of many of the clothes which we wear originated as ideas from a famous fashion house either in Rome, Paris, London, New York or Tokyo. Until the 1950s, Paris was the fashion centre of the world with designers like Dior, Patou and Chanel creating exclusive 'couture' fashion for the wealthy and famous. Today French designers are not the only leaders in fashion. Names like Yuki, Katherine Hamnett, Armani, Karl Lagerfeld, Calvin Klein and Jasper Conran have become household words and their influence on the clothes of ordinary people has been very strong.

In the 1960s, 'couture' clothes lost favour and what we call 'street fashion' dominated. This means that the likes and dislikes of ordinary young people began to influence fashion designers such as Mary Quant and Bill Gibb. Today of course there are still people who can afford beautifully designed and made clothes by important designers. For instance the Princess of Wales has given British fashion design a boost by wearing clothes by a number of young designers like Bruce Oldfield. Nevertheless most of us still get a chance to buy and wear well-designed clothes which are in fashion and suit our purses!

Garment design

Designing garments is the most creative part of the process of garment production. The designer will probably spend a long time thinking, sketching and handling materials. Once ideas have been formed, sketches are produced of the proposed garments together with specifications for construction and details of trimmings, buttons, etc. Samples of suggested fabrics are attached to the sketches and alternative colour schemes might be suggested. Traditionally this is the way in which the designer has worked—with pens, pencils, crayons and fabric samples. This is time-consuming and may be one

DESIGN MATTERS

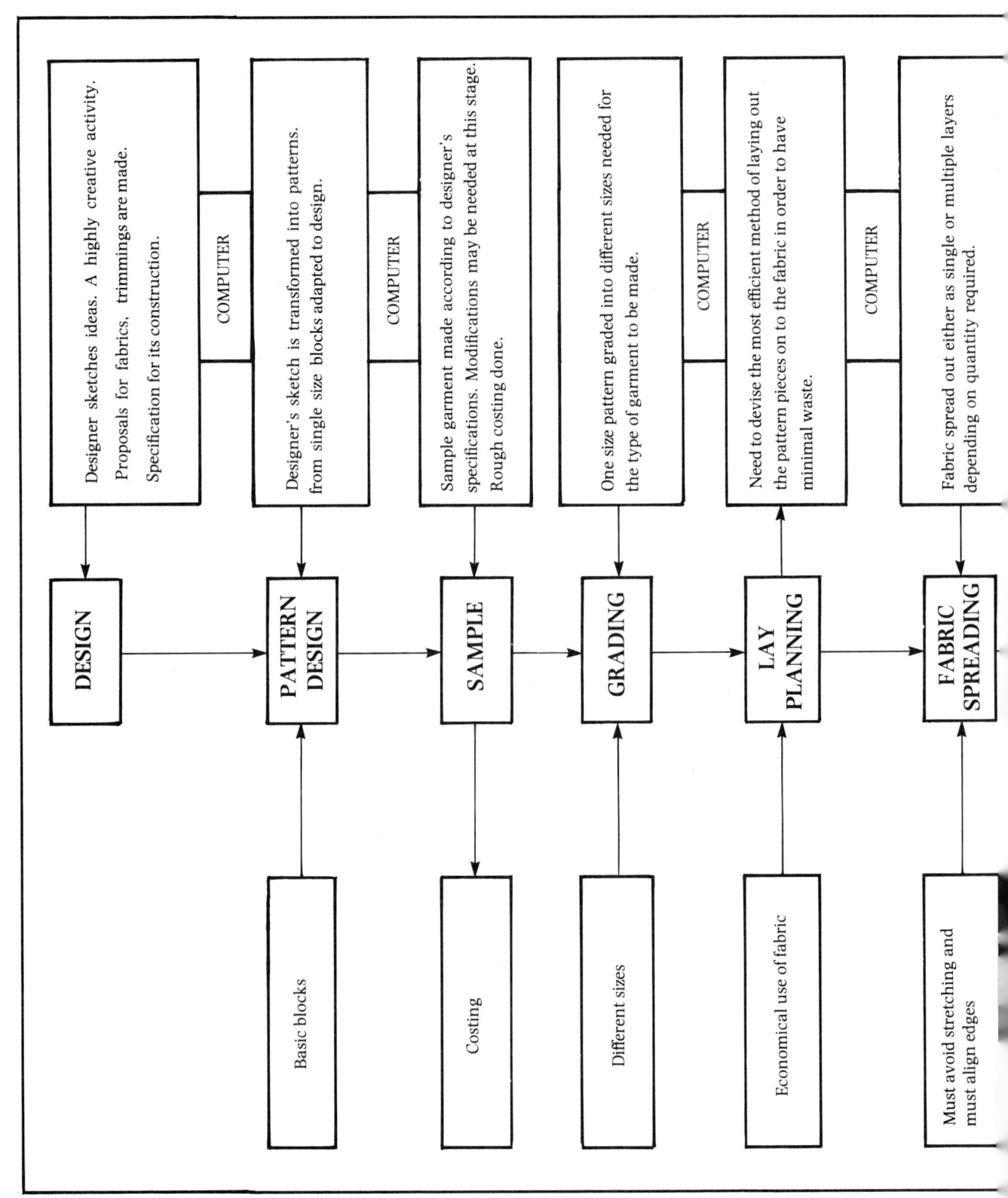

Stage	Description	Tool	Output
DESIGN	Designer sketches ideas. A highly creative activity. Proposals for fabrics, trimmings are made. Specification for its construction.	COMPUTER	
PATTERN DESIGN	Designer's sketch is transformed into patterns from single size blocks adapted to design.	COMPUTER	Basic blocks
SAMPLE	Sample garment made according to designer's specifications. Modifications may be needed at this stage. Rough costing done.		Costing
GRADING	One size pattern graded into different sizes needed for the type of garment to be made.	COMPUTER	Different sizes
LAY PLANNING	Need to devise the most efficient method of laying out the pattern pieces on to the fabric in order to have minimal waste.	COMPUTER	Economical use of fabric
FABRIC SPREADING	Fabric spread out either as single or multiple layers depending on quantity required.		Must avoid stretching and must align edges

Feather motif showing detail of stitchery based on straight stitches by a pupil aged 14 (see pages 73–77) ▶

Detail of Indian embroidery
▼ *showing a variety of stitches (see pages 73–77)*

▲ *Linear machine embroidery on hand-dyed fabric by a 13-year-old pupil (see pages 94–97)*

Appliqué plus stitching by a pupil aged 14
◀ *(see page 87)*

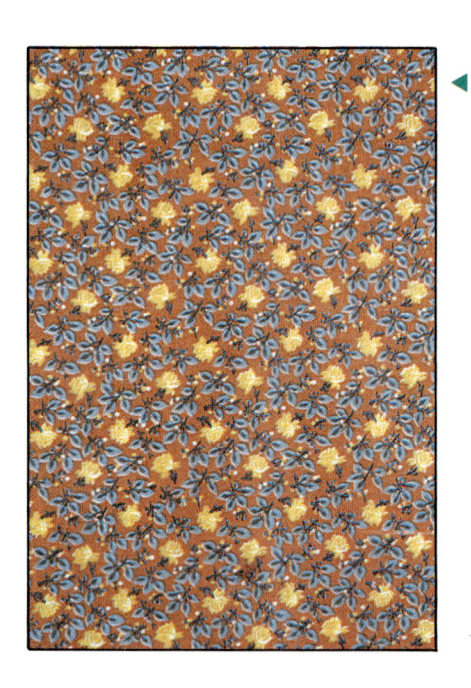

*Variety of commercially printed fabrics
(see pages 98–104)*

THE CLOTHING INDUSTRY

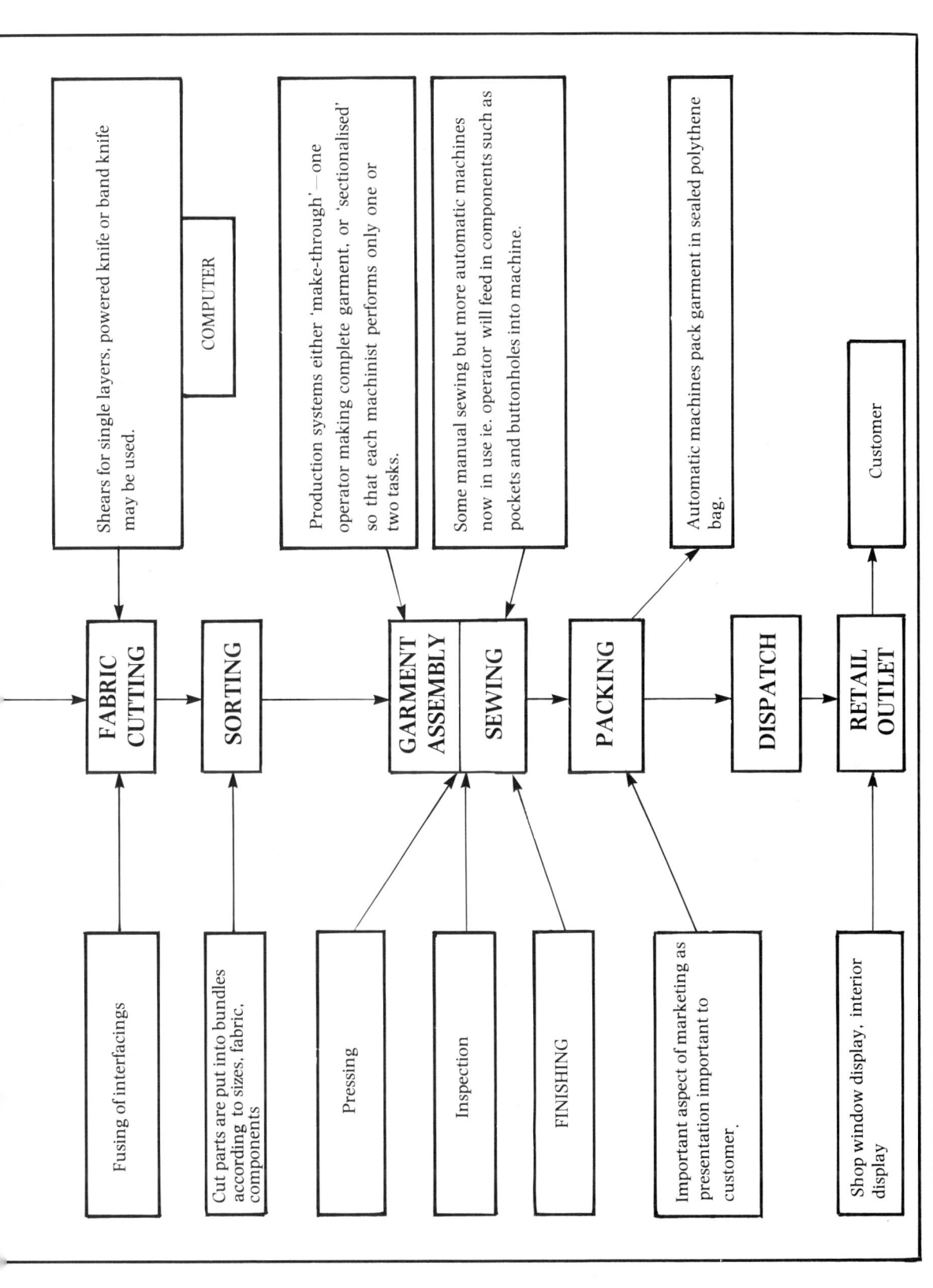

```
Shears for single layers, powered knife or band knife may be used.
           |
           v
    [FABRIC CUTTING] <-- Fusing of interfacings

[COMPUTER]

[FABRIC CUTTING] --> [SORTING] <-- Cut parts are put into bundles according to sizes, fabric, components

[SORTING] --> [GARMENT ASSEMBLY / SEWING]

Production systems either 'make-through' — one operator making complete garment, or 'sectionalised' so that each machinist performs only one or two tasks.

Some manual sewing but more automatic machines now in use ie. operator will feed in components such as pockets and buttonholes into machine.

[GARMENT ASSEMBLY / SEWING] <-- Pressing
[GARMENT ASSEMBLY / SEWING] <-- Inspection
[GARMENT ASSEMBLY / SEWING] <-- FINISHING

[GARMENT ASSEMBLY / SEWING] --> [PACKING]

Automatic machines pack garment in sealed polythene bag.

[PACKING] <-- Important aspect of marketing as presentation important to customer.

[PACKING] --> [DISPATCH] --> [RETAIL OUTLET] --> [Customer]

[RETAIL OUTLET] <-- Shop window display, interior display
```

NOTE: ⬚COMPUTER⬚ This denotes a computer can be used at this stage of the process. There is more about the actual function of the computer in Section 5.

Collar and cuff detail

Black leather

lace

Two eyelet tie

of the reasons why computer aided design (CAD) is used at this point. Section 5 gives more details of the system used.

Once a garment has been sketched, it is handed over to the pattern designers. This also is highly creative work and great skill is needed to translate the sketch into flat, two-dimensional patterns. Again computers are often used at this stage. Once all the pattern pieces are made, a version of the garment can be made up. This is often done in a cheap material like calico and is known as a toile (a sort of calico pattern). The designer and the toile maker work closely together as adjustments to the original design might have to be made. The toile is worn by a model so that fitting can be accurate. Once the toile is corrected, a sample garment can be made up in a chosen fabric and a costing can be done. The designer may still feel that alterations are necessary at this stage.

If the garment concerned is to be of couture standard, then only one version will be made, but if it is to go into mass production, then grading is the next stage. This is a process whereby a variety of sizes of pattern are produced from the one style. The flow chart which follows will explain the process clearly.

In the famous fashion houses mentioned before, the designers will develop a collection of clothes to be shown twice a year, Spring/Summer and Autumn/Winter. These shows are glittering occasions with only specially-invited guests and long-standing customers allowed in. At one time, the launch of a new collection was eagerly awaited but now, with so much fashion news, it does not have quite the same impact. Nevertheless, there is often great excitement at the showing of particular designers' collections because these are often said to be world fashion leaders. Anyone buying direct from a fashion house will have to pay several thousand pounds for a single garment but the rest of us will find that eventually the ideas will come through into the clothes we are able to buy in our local shops.

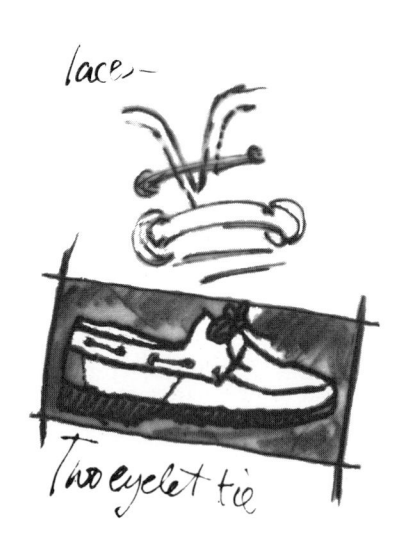

THE CLOTHING INDUSTRY

KEY INVESTIGATION

Your teacher will provide you with some reference material which is about the work of famous fashion designers past and present.

Study the references and make some notes and sketches on any *one* designer's life and work.

ANALYSIS

1. List the key factors that made or make your chosen designer famous.
2. What influences did or does he/she have on the design of everyday clothes?
3. Did or does any particular famous person wear your designer's clothes? If so, is this likely to be influential?

EVALUATION

1. How important do you think fashion designers are?
2. You will see from the flow chart that computers are used quite a bit in the process of designing. Do you think they could take over completely? If so, how?

INVESTIGATION EXTENSION

Design a garment for yourself to be worn for a particular occasion. Produce a design sheet of sketches, fabric samples, and notes about the garment. Good presentation is important.

Work out how much the garment would cost to make.

Let's explore shape creatively

So far in this section, we have concentrated on three-dimensional form (clothes) made from two-dimensional shape (patterns). If you have ever made a garment from a paper pattern, you will have a good understanding of how this all works. But of course clothes are not the only thing that can be made using flat shapes sewn together. Toys, patchwork, bags, cushions and many other items are made using the same principle. Toys and dolls are delightful small articles to make by both beginners and more experienced sewers.

To start with it is important to know for whom the toy is intended. The age of the child is an important consideration as is the safety of the toy. Choice of suitable materials, colours, textures and weight must be given importance when planning to make a toy.

Small, soft toys make ideal playthings for a young child and can often be adapted for use as a decorative article for your own room. Simple shapes are often the most versatile, are not too difficult to put together, and may be decorated in many different ways. Cubes, 'humbugs' and cylinders make good shapes to start with.

These shapes make excellent soft toys or mobiles for children yet can be enlarged to make articles suitable for your own use.

KEY INVESTIGATION

1 Cut some thin paper into six equal-sized squares about 20 cm × 20 cm to make patterns for a cube toy.
2 Decide on a simple design theme, such as animals, flowers or clowns' faces and collect relevant resource material to help you.
3 Sketch six different versions of your chosen theme, one for each side of the cube.
4 Using reference books, look up techniques that might be suitable to carry out your design theme. Make notes on these.

ANALYSIS

1 Work out a colour scheme suitable for the toy, making reference to the particular design theme you have chosen.
2 Decide on suitable materials in which to make the cube toy.
3 Decide on a particular technique to use for the decoration based on the facilities and materials available, but use this as an opportunity to develop your skills and knowledge of textile crafts.
4 Once these decisions have been made, go ahead and decorate each of the six squares. Sew them together to form a cube and decide on a suitable filling to help it keep its shape.

EVALUATION

You should now be able to see for yourself how two-dimensional shapes can be put together to construct a three-dimensional form.
1 Did you find it difficult to make up the cube? If so, what points will you remember when doing a similar exercise again?
2 Why do you think it is important to keep to one colour scheme and one design theme for each side of the cube?
3 Do you think you could now make a pattern for a more complicated shape? Try to work out how you could make a soft ball, a cylindrical draught excluder or 'humbug' pin cushion.

SHAPE

INVESTIGATION EXTENSION

1. Using fruits as your design theme, design and make a number of small Christmas tree decorations using felt, beads and sequins with some hand stitchery.
2. Design and make a cosy for a coffee pot or tea pot that you have at home. Choose suitable materials and decoration to match your kitchen colour scheme.

Shape from the environment

ENVIRONMENT INTERACTION

So far, we have concentrated on finding out how three-dimensional shape is created. It is important to look also at shapes that can be used as flat patterns. There are examples of such shapes all around us. Such shapes are extremely versatile and can be used effectively for appliqué (see page 87), quilted designs, canvas stitchery, knitted designs and fabric printed patterns.

One important rule to remember when you are creating design of this type, is to relate the shapes within the design itself to the overall shape of the article. For example, the shape, size and proportion of the motif on the bib of this child's dungarees (see margin) must be related to the bib itself, and to the whole garment.

Here is another example. The knitted shapes on this jumper (see margin) must bear a relationship to the jumper itself.

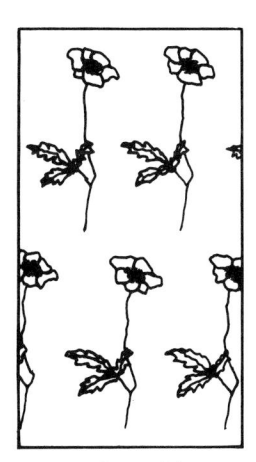

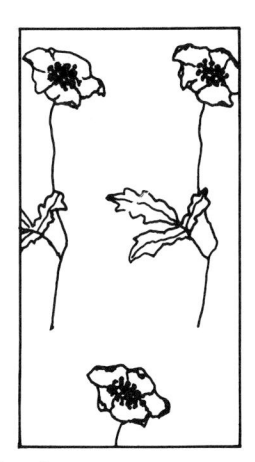

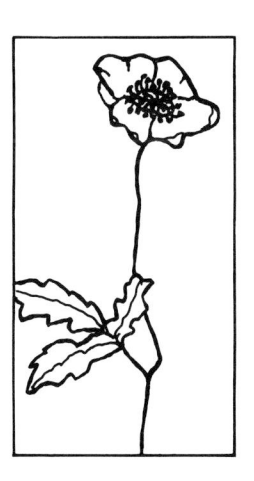

Designs for wall-hangings based on poppies

If you look above at the drawings based on poppies you will see how very different the three versions look although the shapes are the same in each.

DESIGN MATTERS

What have you discovered about the relationship of the motif itself to the outer shape of the wall-hangings?

Firstly, you will probably see that very small shapes appear to 'float' and do not have any connection with the frame. Very large shapes seem cramped and crowded and do not have enough 'breathing' space around them. A good balance is achieved when the shapes of motif and frame are related to give attention to each.

In designers' language, the poppies are said to be positive shapes, and the background, the negative shape. Both positive and negative shapes are equally important in design and must be given consideration. We generally are more concerned with the positive shapes and neglect to think about backgrounds.

Try the following exercise.

Draw two rectangles of the same size, about 5 cm × 3 cm. Cut another rectangle of the same size but in coloured paper. Out of this, cut the initial of your first name. Cut the shape out removing as few pieces as you can. Look at the examples in the margin to help you.

In the first of your rectangles, put the letter itself, stick it down. In the second rectangle put all the pieces of coloured paper that you cut off from *around* your initial, stick these down in the right order. Look at the two designs in the margin. You will see that you can read the initial in both rectangles.

This shows that both positive and negative shapes are equally important in a design.

This can be a very easy way of adding an individual touch to your work. If you use the same system and cut your whole name out of felt you can easily stick or machine-sew the pieces down to create a personal 'designer' touch to your bag, anorak or pencil case.

KEY INVESTIGATION

1. Make a collection of pictures of similar objects, e.g. cats or vehicles. You will find examples of these in colour supplements and magazines. Sometimes, the best examples are to be found in the backgrounds of advertisements. If you collect postcards or old birthday cards these also might be useful.
2. Place tracing paper over the pictures and trace off the shapes of the objects you have identified.
3. Using a set square, frame each shape by drawing a rectangle around the tracing.

▷ ANALYSIS

1 Which of the designs you have traced seems to have the best balance of positive and negative shapes?
2 Which of the designs you have traced has a good contrast of large and smaller shapes?

◻ EVALUATION

1 What do you understand by 'balance' in design?
2 How have you made use of positive and negative shapes?
3 What other techniques might you have used to carry out this particular design?

INVESTIGATION EXTENSION

Develop a design for machine-stitched appliqué which uses an enlarged version of the best of your traced designs. Use a colour scheme of your choice in printed and plain fabrics. (See below for details of this technique known as appliqué.)

Fabric appliqué

Appliqué is a technique where shapes of one colour are cut out and sewn on to a contrast fabric. It is an excellent technique to use for motifs on clothing, wall-hangings, cushions and many other decorative articles.

Two examples of fabric appliqué

DESIGN MATTERS

The problem with traditional methods of appliqué was in the control of fraying edges and in cutting out quite complicated shapes cleanly and accurately. If you can use some of the modern non-woven textiles, fabric appliqué can be much simplified.

There are three simple ways of doing this.

A Using iron-on interfacing (Vilene).
B Using Stitch 'n' Tear.
C Using Bondaweb.

EFFICIENCY

KEY INVESTIGATION

1 Sketch a number of leaf shapes using references available. Select one shape and draw it on thin paper to use as a template (no larger than 9 cm × 6 cm).
2 Cut out three rectangles of calico each 15 cm × 10 cm
3 Choose a piece of contrasting cotton fabric, printed or plain, from which to cut your leaf shapes. Do not cut out the shapes at this stage.
4 Take one piece of calico in turn and apply a leaf shape using the following methods.

Method A   Using Iron-on Interfacing   (Vilene medium weight)

1 Take a small piece of the contrast fabric and iron on a piece of Vilene on the wrong side.
2 Place your leaf-shaped template on the wrong side, draw around it and cut it out with sharp scissors.
3 Place the fabric leaf wrong side down on one piece of calico and pin then tack it into place.
4 Machine around the leaf shape using a medium-sized zigzag stitch (stitch length—0.5: stitch width—3).

Method B   Using Stitch 'n' Tear

1 Cut a leaf shape out of the contrast fabric using the template as before.
2 Cut out a rectangle of Stitch 'n' Tear and place it on the calico.
3 Place the leaf shape on top of the stitch 'n' tear and pin then tack it on through all layers.
4 Machine around the leaf shape using a medium-sized zigzag stitch as before.
5 When machining is complete, tear away the Stitch 'n' Tear.

Method C   Using Bondaweb

1 Take a piece of contrast fabric and iron Bondaweb on the back of it.

2. Take the leaf template, place it on the paper side of the Bondaweb and draw around it with a pencil.
3. Cut out the leaf shape and peel off the paper backing.
4. Place the leaf shape wrong side down on the calico and iron it into place.
5. Machine around the leaf shape as before.

ANALYSIS

Record the results of the three investigations on a table as shown below:

	Time taken	Degree of difficulty	Problems arising	Results
Method A				
Method B				
Method C				

EVALUATION

1. Which method proved most satisfactory?
2. How could you overcome any problems you encountered?
3. Using reference books provided, look up a traditional method of working appliqué.
    What improvements do you think the use of modern bonded textiles makes to the practical use of appliqué?

INVESTIGATION EXTENSION

1. Trains and carriages are popular with young children. Design a border pattern, using bright colours which could be appliquéd on to an article of children's clothing.
2. Design a panel for your room based on hot-air balloons soaring high into the sky. Use mainly appliqué to capture this very colourful spectacle.
3. Sweaters and cardigans which are decorated with satin appliqué are popular and attractive, but many are very expensive. Design a suitable decoration to enhance a plain article you already have or one which you could knit. Use a suitable method of applying the satin appliqué. You may add sequins and beads.

4 You have been given a satin cushion with a lace edging which looks very plain when in place. You have decided to decorate it with butterflies. Use your machine skills and hand stitchery as well as appliqué when producing your design. Appliqué two butterflies on the cushion using a suitable method and attach the third butterfly so that it stands away from the surface.

LET'S LOOK AT THE USE OF LINE IN DESIGN

AESTHETICS

We have already investigated colour and texture, shape and form. These elements of design in textiles are obviously important because they are actually part of each and every textile we use. Every textile is coloured in one way or another and every textile has a surface which can be described as its texture. In addition you will have carried out some work which further explores shape and form.

The study of 'line' in design is not so easy to understand. We can explore the meaning of line in textile design in two ways. One way is to look at the way in which lines can be used as design in themselves. The other way has a much broader meaning and refers to the style features of a garment or other article. For instance, we say that a sofa has long low lines or a skirt, a flared line.

Let's look at what line means in terms of fashion in textiles. In clothing there have been in the past some very dominant 'lines'. If you look at any pictures of historical costume, for example, you will see how the shapes of garments for both men and women have changed over the years. In the past this change has been slow, probably over a period of many decades, whereas today, as you will know, fashion change is very rapid. New 'lines' are constantly coming into the shops. From the turn of this century to the 1960s,

French fashion designers more or less dictated fashion in Europe. Of course, their clothes were very expensive and only available to the few wealthy people who could afford them. Nevertheless, their influence was felt by ordinary people in that copies were made which appeared in the nation's shops. Of course, these copies could not be the same as the originals. The latter would have been made in the most expensive materials and made as exclusive 'one-offs'. The clothes that appeared in the ordinary shops were mass-produced and made of poorer-quality materials but, the 'line', that is, the main style features and silhouette, were the same, so that ordinary consumers could, in time, have garments quite like the exclusive clothes of the very rich and famous. One designer, Christian Dior, led the fashion world until his death in 1958, and his work became nicknamed by the style lines invented. You may have heard of the A line, the H line and so on.

It is interesting to study the style lines of modern fashion. The same 'ingredients' are still there—silhouette, shape, line.

KEY INVESTIGATION

1. Collect some up-to-date pictures of clothes that appeal to you. These could come from magazines or advertisements.
2. Place tracing paper over the illustrations and trace off the silhouettes and the main style lines that you can see.
3. Trace these line drawings off on to plain paper and go over them with a strong felt pen line.

ANALYSIS

1. Which features in the clothes you have studied gave *strong* style lines?
2. Take a garment that you own such as a dress, jacket or coat and analyse its style lines by making a sketch of the back and front views.

EVALUATION

1. How do you think style lines could be used to improve figure faults?
2. Taking style line into consideration, why do you choose the clothes you do?

INVESTIGATION EXTENSION

1. Take several pieces of striped material and experiment to see how you can change the appearance of the fabric. You could enhance the stripes by using stitchery (machine or hand), adding braids or bias binding, etc. Try pleating or cutting and pinning the fabric. Suggest suitable uses for each of your experiments.
2. Take a piece of striped fabric, cut it into squares or rectangles and re-arrange the pieces, then re-join them to make an interesting pattern from the stripes. Make the new fabric into a bag you would find useful to your needs.
3. You can use stripes as a useful aid for gathering fabric for such work as smocking. Take a piece of narrow striped fabric about 45 cm wide by 15 cm long so that the lines are vertical. Work several rows of gathering stitches using the lines as a guide. Pull up all the gathers, note how the fabric is reduced in width. Embroider the smocking stitches. Remove gathering threads. Suggest where this type of work could be used on clothing.
4. Using fabric with wider stripes work out how you could smock a cushion to give the surface a textured effect. Use the stripes to advantage.

Take a look at stripes

As we have noted, a study of style lines is important particularly when we are choosing and making garments for ourselves but this is not the only important use of line in design.

Lines on fabrics can cover the surface with stripes of various widths, can form borders or be used to emphasise and outline. Take a look at a pair of training shoes and see how many linear features are used. Think of all the fabrics and wall coverings we have in our homes which are striped or have borders.

ENVIRONMENT INTERACTION

Stripes are lines, which may be thick, thin, straight, wavy or zigzagged. In between each stripe is a space, which may be wide or narrow. Stripes are used in nature by animals, birds, insects and fish and by plants and also in mineral formations. Under the earth's surface there are many layers of rock known as strata. As the sea comes in, its waves form curving lines on the beach and as it goes out it leaves a pattern of lines in the sand. Perhaps the most beautiful uses of line in nature are those used by animals as a form of protection or camouflage, the skins of the zebra and tiger being perhaps the most beautiful forms of this. It is fascinating to see how many variations there are on a basic stripe pattern. No two zebras are alike!

KEY INVESTIGATION

1. Collect pictures of examples of stripes used in nature from animal, vegetable and mineral sources. Use colour supplements and magazines and trace examples from library books.
2. Using crayons, felt pens or cut paper, record the patterns of the stripes that you have found. Label your work and describe each in full.

ANALYSIS

Make a table which shows how each of the examples uses stripes.

	Source	*Description*
Animal	Zebra	*Broad black curvy stripes on white body. Stripes thick on body, thinner on legs*
Vegetable		
Mineral		

EVALUATION

1. Write a short paragraph which explains why stripe designs are successful in nature.
2. List the points that you could apply to your own work in textiles.

INVESTIGATION EXTENSION

Carry out the following design brief using one or more of the stripe patterns you have collected.

Make a design in two colours only which could be printed on a summer shirt. Sketch the shirt showing the print in use.

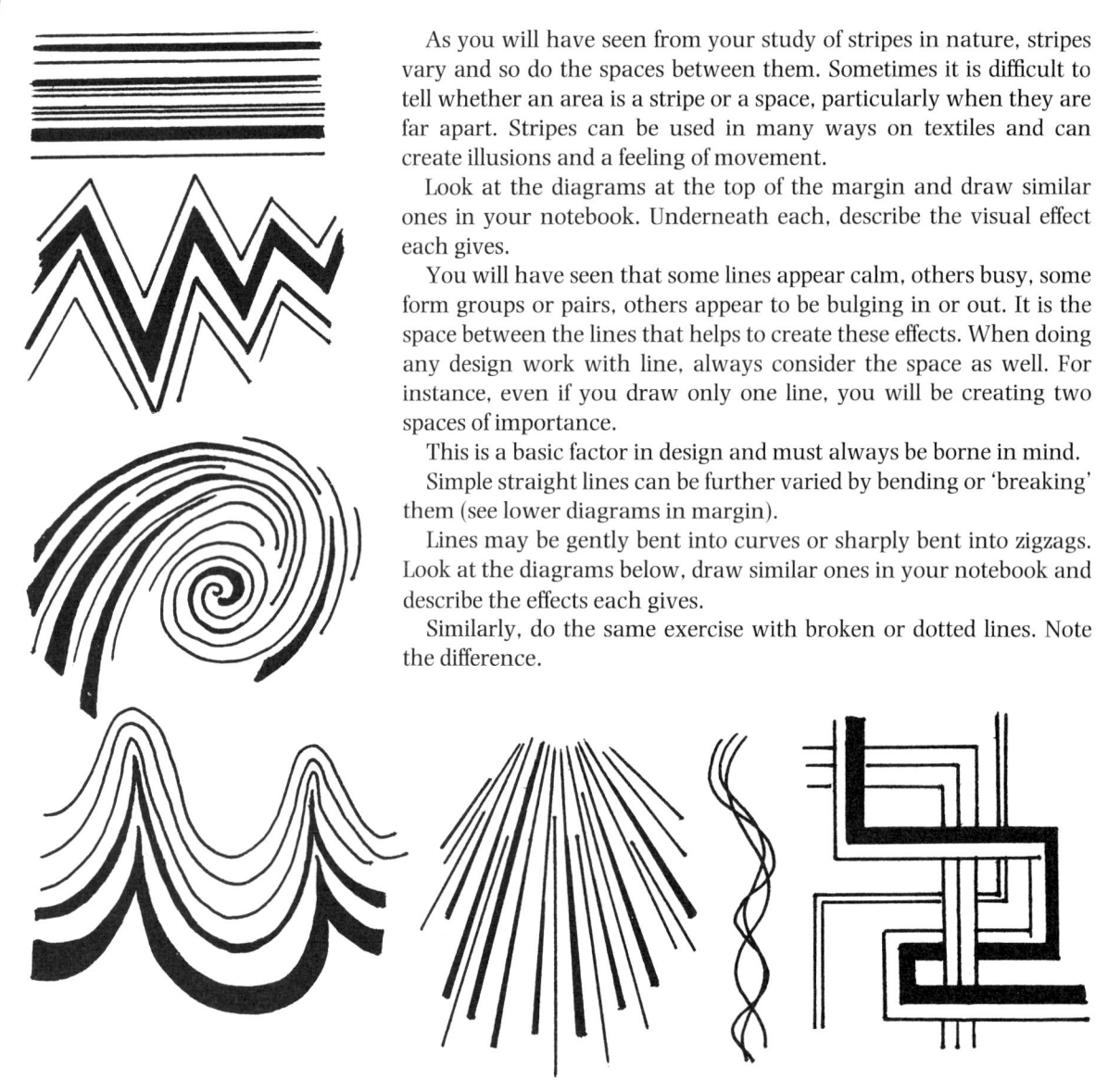

As you will have seen from your study of stripes in nature, stripes vary and so do the spaces between them. Sometimes it is difficult to tell whether an area is a stripe or a space, particularly when they are far apart. Stripes can be used in many ways on textiles and can create illusions and a feeling of movement.

Look at the diagrams at the top of the margin and draw similar ones in your notebook. Underneath each, describe the visual effect each gives.

You will have seen that some lines appear calm, others busy, some form groups or pairs, others appear to be bulging in or out. It is the space between the lines that helps to create these effects. When doing any design work with line, always consider the space as well. For instance, even if you draw only one line, you will be creating two spaces of importance.

This is a basic factor in design and must always be borne in mind.

Simple straight lines can be further varied by bending or 'breaking' them (see lower diagrams in margin).

Lines may be gently bent into curves or sharply bent into zigzags. Look at the diagrams below, draw similar ones in your notebook and describe the effects each gives.

Similarly, do the same exercise with broken or dotted lines. Note the difference.

Linear patterns on the sewing machine

The stripe or line is extremely versatile as an element of design. One of the easiest ways of using it is to create a linear pattern using a sewing machine.

TECHNOLOGY

Some machines will only sew a straight stitch, others will zigzag, others may have a number of cams built into them which will allow them to produce decorative lines of stitchery. It is a good idea to start some experimental machine stitchery using straight stitch and zigzag stitch only.

LINEAR PATTERNS ON THE SEWING MACHINE

EFFICIENCY

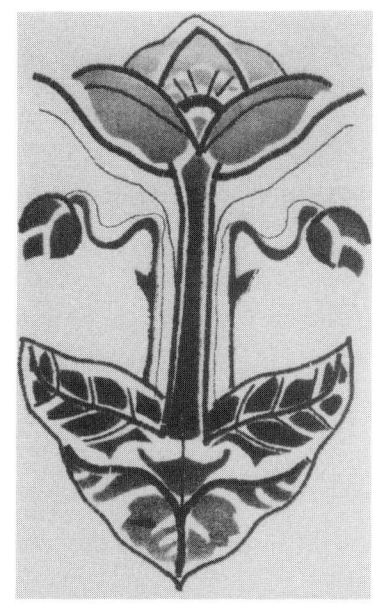

Using simple linear designs, you can build up very attractive patterns which can be worked on fabric either by hand or by the use of machine stitches. Because of the nature of the machine, its stitches are effective and easy to work in a combination of straight lines, gentle curves or angles and corners. This seems rather limiting as far as design is concerned but the results can be made more interesting if braids, ribbons and lace are used applied with machine stitches. Colour may also be introduced in the form of dye painting, transfer or other printing techniques. Machine stitches can look very beautiful and elegant in a design and your simple experiments should begin to give you an idea of how versatile linear stitching can be.

KEY INVESTIGATION

Look at some of the sketches you have made using straight, curvy and zigzag lines. Choose three or four of the most interesting ones and carry these out on *double* fabric* using one colour only.

a Mark out three or four 10 cm squares on plain fabric using a fabric marker.

b Transfer the chosen linear designs to the fabric with a marker pen or felt pens.

c Fill in the design using either straight stitch or an open zigzag stitch (stitch length—1·5: stitch width—3).

* *On double fabric you will be able to get a better stitch tension.*

Linear machine embroidery on a stencil print

ANALYSIS

1 How difficult did you find this exercise? What caused you most difficulties? How could you improve your machine skills?
2 Which of your designs proved to be the most effective and why?
3 Which of your designs proved to be the least effective and why?

EVALUATION

1 Suggest ways in which the exercises could be made more visually interesting.
2 Suggest ways in which your simple linear stitched patterns might be used to decorate clothing for children. Sketch your ideas.
3 Suggest ways in which they might be used to decorate a square cushion cover. Sketch your ideas.

INVESTIGATION EXTENSION

1 Design a panel to be hung in a Field Study Centre. Base your idea on a landscape, woodland scene or river scene. Spray dyes or fabric crayons or paints may help you to build up the design. Use your sewing machine to add the detail to the panel.

2 Design a wall-hanging for an architect's office, basing your design on the interesting patterns made by scaffolding. Include some corded quilting to give a raised effect.
3 Your young brother has an old chest in which to keep his toys, and it needs to be covered when not in use. Design a cover for this chest and base the decoration on exploding fireworks.

Free Machine Stitching

For complete freedom to stitch lines in any direction we must either work by hand or use free machine embroidery.

EFFICIENCY

SAFETY

This is a most exciting technique and well worth trying providing you are very aware of safety aspects. Your teacher will give you full instructions and probably demonstrate how it is done but the basic rules are these:
1 Remove the sewing foot.
2 Lower the feed (your machine handbook will show you how to do these two operations).
3 Mount your fabric tightly in an embroidery ring frame.
4 Thread up the machine.
5 Turn the balance wheel towards you and bring up the spool thread so that both top and bottom threads are visible on the surface of the fabric before starting to sew.
6 Always lower the presser foot lever although there is no foot there.
7 Think safety! Keep your fingers clear of the needle.

KEY INVESTIGATION

1 Set up a machine for free machine embroidery.
2 Take a piece of white cotton fabric and sketch on it a simple design using a continuous line of vertical, horizontal and diagonal lines. Ensure that the design will fit the embroidery frame available and use the idea of buildings as your theme. Use a coloured pencil or felt pen.
3 Thread the machine with No. 40 cotton in a colour that will show up clearly.
4 Thread the spool with the same type of thread but in another colour.
5 Stretch the fabric tightly in the frame—it should be 'drum' tight (test it with your fingers).
6 Turn the balance wheel so that the needle is at its highest point. Slide the frame under the needle so that the fabric is flat on the machine bed. Position the needle point so that it is ready to start sewing on one of the vertical lines of your design.
7 Turn the balance wheel towards you so that the needle enters the fabric once and comes out once bringing the spool thread up to the top surface.

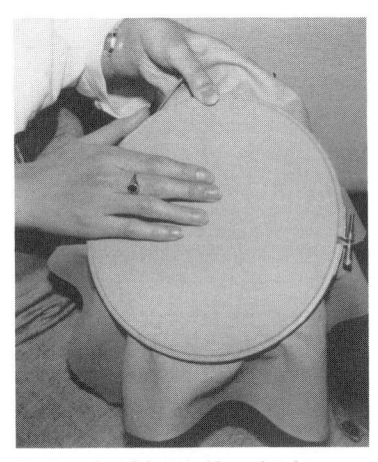

Testing that fabric is 'drum' tight

FREE MACHINE STITCHING

If the spool thread does not come up, it is usually a sign that the fabric is not tight enough in the frame so take it out and start again.

8 At a slow speed, start to stitch over the lines you have drawn on the fabric. You will find the vertical lines easy to do as this is the normal movement of the work through the machine. When you come to stitch over the horizontal and diagonal lines do not turn the frame but move it according to the direction of the lines of the design. Once you have got over your fear of sewing in this way, you will understand why this technique is called 'free' machine embroidery.
9 Once all the lines have been embroidered, go over some of them more than once to build up an interesting framework on which to develop your design.
10 Experiment by filling in the shapes you have created. You will find that the freely drawn linear patterns are very beautiful and not too difficult to do with practice.
11 If you like, you can add some freely worked zigzag stitches to your design.

▷ ANALYSIS

1 What are the main differences between the normal use of the machine and using it for 'free' work?
2 What did you find the most difficult to do?
3 List the main points of safety that you must be aware of.
4 Why is this technique so useful for linear designs?

☐ EVALUATION

Write a short article for your school or club magazine which describes free machine embroidery and encourages other people, who don't usually enjoy sewing, to try it for themselves.

INVESTIGATION EXTENSION

From the results of your experiments, develop your skills by trying the following design briefs.

1 You have decided to use your newly-acquired skill of free machining to make designs for your own greetings cards. Base your ideas on some of the following: feathers, flames of a fire, waves, a weeping willow, grasses, interesting-shaped leaves. Work out two or three ideas and place them in card mounts.
2 Faces and hair make interesting subjects for free machining. Make a collection of interesting subjects—pop stars, politicians, famous people, etc., which you could use as a basis for design.

97

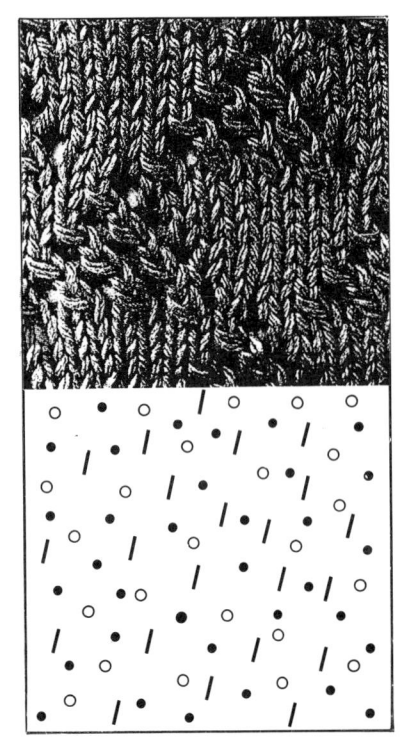

LET'S LOOK AT PATTERN

What is pattern? Pattern is simply the repetition of a unit of design. Patterns may be regular and formal, such as in evenly-placed railings around a building or the regular placing of bricks to build a wall. Pattern may also be irregular and informal, such as in the spread of daisies growing in a lawn or a pile of books lying on a shelf.

Pattern is very important in textiles. You will have already been aware of pattern when you examined woven and knitted fabric in Section 2.

Here, the structure of the fabric itself and the pattern of interlocked stitches in knitting or interlaced threads in weaving are inseparable. The placing of bricks in a wall can be described as pattern and structure: for without the regular pattern of bricks there can be no wall!

Pattern was also an important element when we looked at fabric textures—you could think of some textural surfaces as miniature patterns such as the tiny loops in towelling. In free machine embroidery and hand stitchery, for example, pattern making was also part of what was happening on the fabric.

How many different patterns can you see here?

Cherry blossom—random pattern (left)
Victorian Palm House—formal pattern (right)

Pattern networks

It would be impossible to produce the kind of fabric we need for our clothing and our homes without taking into account the way in which the design is repeated on the fabric's surface. Because virtually

EFFICIENCY

all printed fabric is mass-produced nowadays, a number of rules for designing fabric prints have to be obeyed. In previous centuries much of the fabric produced was hand printed but the same rules applied.

In order to print fabric economically, it is necessary to organise the design within the finished width of the fabric. If a fabric that is to be printed is 90 cm wide, then the designer of the print must make sure that the unit of design to be used will fit into that width. The length of the unit is not so important as many hundreds of metres of fabric are made at one time.

In order to make the units cover the fabric regularly, a certain system must be used. These systems are often called pattern networks.

Let us look at these networks.

Square Network

The simplest one is the square network. It consists of regular repeats of a unit across and down the fabric. Check patterns follow this network.

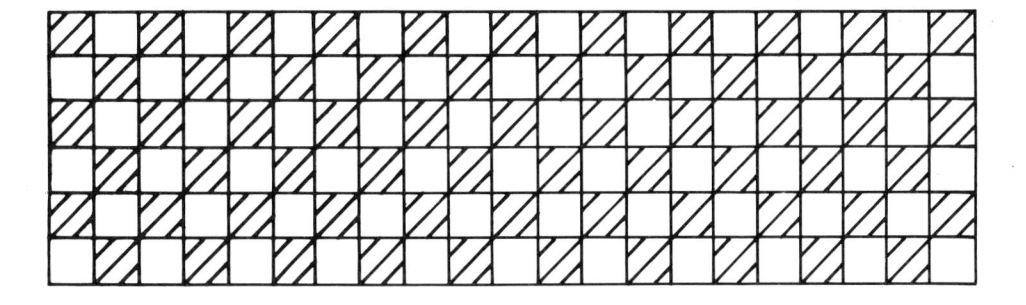

Half Drop Network

The most common design network used for printed fabric for both clothing and household uses is the half drop network.

This interlocks the units of the design and makes a more flowing overall design. Also it can appear to build up interesting diagonal lines across the fabric. This pattern network is used for both small and large designs.

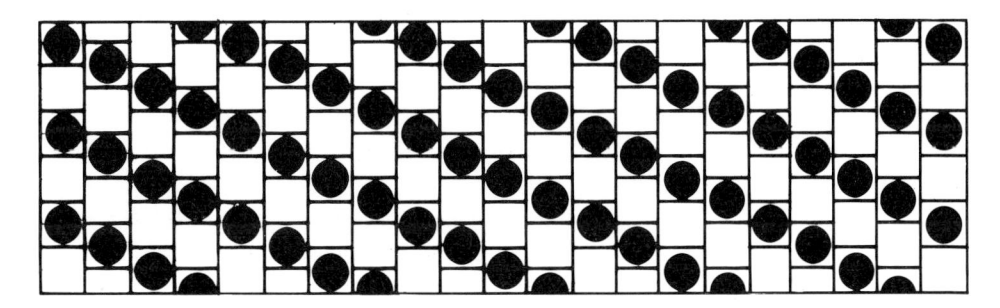

Brick Network

The brick network is very similar to the half drop except that it works across the fabric horizontally rather than vertically, just like the bricks in a wall.

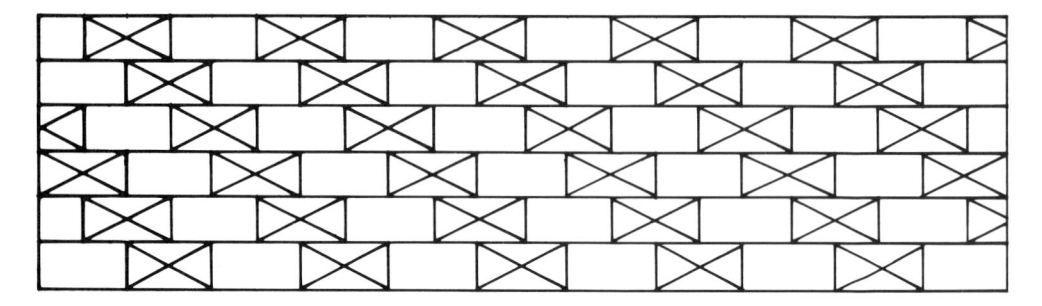

Stripes and Borders

Many printed textiles have simple patterns of stripes. Stripes may run across the fabric horizontally or run down it vertically, and less often diagonally. Stripes are often common patterns in knitting, e.g. cable patterns, Fair Isle and fisherman's rib.

Stripes may be of solid colour and be either narrow or broad; in mixed colours and widths or made up of many smaller patterns put together.

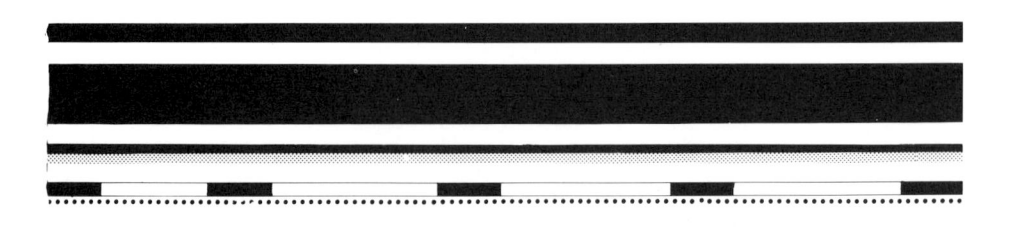

Borders are usually wide stripes which are printed so that when the fabric is used, the patterned border will form a distinctive edge to the article. Sheets, tea towels, curtains, skirts and scarves often have printed border patterns.

KEY INVESTIGATION

1. Make a list of all the printed textiles you have in your home and in your wardrobe.
2. Put your results in a table as shown below.

Article	Type of print	Number of colours used	Source of design
Duvet cover	Border	Blue, grey, yellow (3)	Geometric

3. Find out what 'colourway' means.
4. Find out what 'mix and match' means.

ANALYSIS

Bring in one article from home which has a printed design on it.

1. Examine the article and see if you can find where the repeat of the unit begins and ends.
2. Make a drawing, actual size, of the unit of design. Colour it in.

EVALUATION

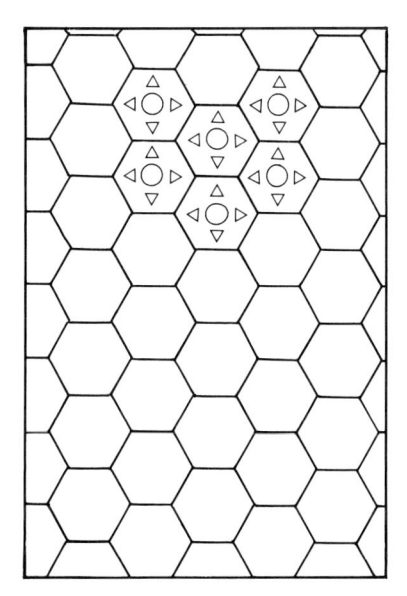

1. How important do you think the size of the printed unit is? Describe the relationship between the size of the printed unit and the function of the article you brought in.
2. How important do you think colour is in printed textile design?
3. Why do you think printed textiles are so popular in the home today?

In addition to the pattern networks we have already examined, there are a few more less common ones. These are particularly beautiful and may remind you of patchwork and other patterns.

Hexagon

This is the method of putting together units of design which are six sided. It is often used in nature to produce strong and very beautiful structures such as honeycomb. Bees make this out of wax and use the structure in which to lay their eggs. You may have seen honeycomb, it is sometimes put into jars of clear honey, it is quite edible and is supposed to have medicinal powers.

Shell

This is another that you will recognise. The shell network is made up of interlocking curves resembling cockleshells. In nature this network may be seen in fish scales and birds' feathers. The shell-shaped unit is made by overlapping circles as in the diagram below.

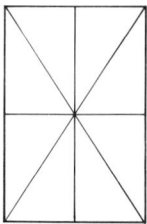

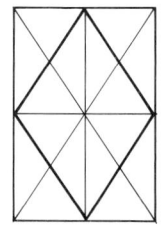

Ogee

This is a beautiful curving network which is made up of 'S'-shaped units. To understand how it works, it is worth drawing one.

Stage 1
Draw a rectangle of any size you like.

Stage 2
Draw in diagonal lines and centre lines.

Stage 3
Draw in a diamond shape.

Stage 4
Drawn in 'S'-shaped lines across the four sides of the diamond. If you find this difficult, draw one accurately and then trace it off.

This network is often used for printed designs on curtain material and for loose covers. It is often used for very large repeat patterns and when the shapes are full of decoration in full colour, the results are rich and exotic.

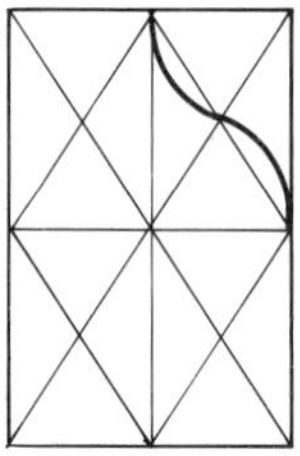

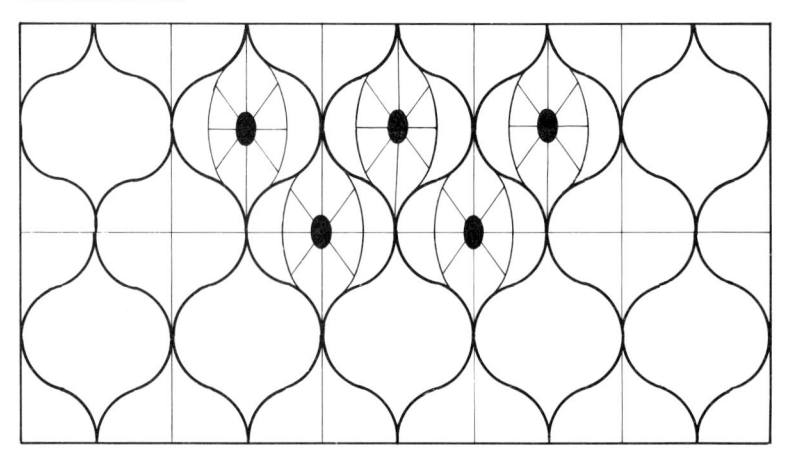

PATTERN NETWORKS

KEY INVESTIGATION

HUMAN DEVELOPMENT
EFFICIENCY

Using the references your teacher has provided, read about the history and technique of patchwork. Answer the following questions.
1. What is patchwork?
2. Why was it so important not to waste fabric?
3. In what way is modern patchwork different from early patchwork?
4. Which design networks are used for patchwork as well as for printed textiles?

ANALYSIS

Patchwork is a craft that uses pattern in a unique way. Using your references find examples where:
1. the fabrics used are already printed with a pattern,
2. the shapes form a distinctive pattern when they are stitched together,
3. the arrangement of colours, tones, patterned and plain fabrics forms yet another pattern.

EVALUATION

1. Why do you think patchwork patterns of the past and present are so successful?
2. What are the key factors involved in a successful patchwork design?

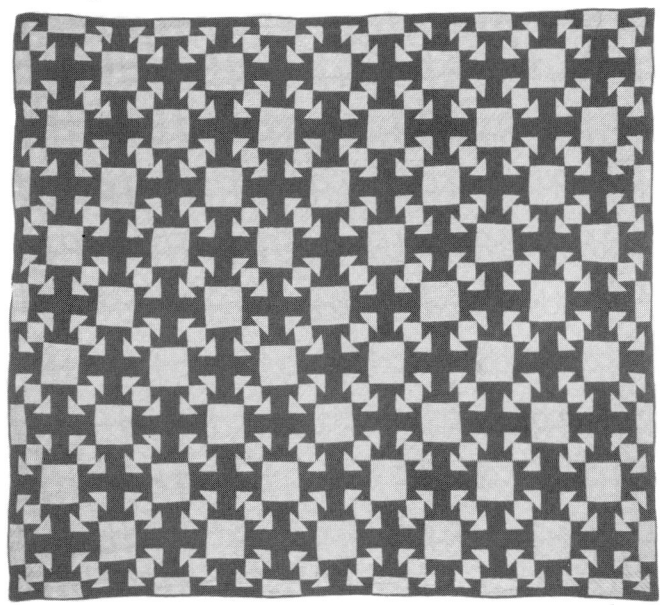

Patchwork, Ulster 19th century
Collection of Lynda Kavanagh

INVESTIGATION EXTENSION

1. Your mother leaves her knitting about the house and you have decided to make her a patchwork bag to contain it. Design the bag which would meet her needs and then complete sufficient patchwork to make up the bag.
2. Your sister is due to have a baby in the near future and has asked you to make a pram quilt. Using patchwork, design and plan a suitable quilt. You may wish to add some appliqué or embroidery to the patchwork before making up the quilt.
3. There is curtain material left over from your new multicoloured bedroom curtains and you wish to make some scatter cushions to match. By careful cutting you could make the cushions in log-cabin patchwork.

Log-cabin Patchwork

This type of patchwork was named after the early American technique of constructing simple cabins from logs chopped down from the forests. The patchwork traditionally has a patch of bright colour in the centre of the square which represents the fire. Around the 'fire', strips of fabric are arranged, two dark and two light in tone, these represent the flickering light and shadows cast by the fire.

4

Consumer Awareness

LET'S CONSIDER TEXTILES AND THE CONSUMER

AESTHETICS

You will have been aware throughout this book that textiles are essential to our lives. In order to meet all our needs, textiles have to vary in type, characteristics, design and of course, performance. In the last section we looked at design and the individual elements that are relevant to textiles, shape and form, line, colour and texture, and pattern. Throughout the investigations, you will have noticed that you cannot actually separate these elements from fabric construction and its eventual function. For instance, when you are making patchwork, you are involved in using the design elements of colour, shape and pattern and are using woven cotton fabrics to make something beautiful and useful, perhaps a cushion. When working free machine embroidery, you are using the design elements of line, colour, texture and pattern to create delicate designs suitable for a number of different purposes. Make a table like the one below to include all the practical pieces of work you have completed.

Technique	Shape/form	Line	Colour	Texture	Pattern	Function
Patchwork	✓		✓		✓	Cushion
Free machine embroidery		✓	✓	✓	✓	Monogrammed badge

EFFICIENCY
AESTHETICS

SAFETY

All the textiles that people young or old use for any purpose have been designed. All the design elements that we have been looking at should be considered when we buy textiles. Textile designers are trained to put together these elements in ways which are appropriate to the future function and performance of each finished fabric or textile article. For example, designers of printed fabric for household use will make sure that the product they design is suitable for its function in the home, that it looks good and is acceptable to members of the public. Such fabrics must be available in different colourways, be competitively priced, safe to use, easy to care for and attractive to look at. What do you think designers of children's clothes should ensure? Cut out a picture of a child's outfit, stick it in your notebook and list all the things that you think the designer of the outfit was concerned with.

Fashion is always changing and the average consumer today is more aware of these changes than ever before. The mass media—TV, newspapers and magazines—help keep us up to date with latest trends across the world. Designers from Europe, America and Japan will have an influence on the clothes we wear, and the fabrics which we use in our homes.

Fashion in the past changed very slowly, it could have taken a hundred years or more for a new style to travel across Europe or a newly-discovered technique to become widely accepted and used. This was because communication between countries was slow and often hazardous. Travel was only undertaken by the few wealthy people who were able to be accompanied by bodyguards, or merchants who were anxious to trade. These were the people prepared to take risks to discover what was going on outside their own country. Of course, there was no photography until comparatively recent times. Only the wealthy and members of the upper classes ever saw portraits of people wearing new styles or had a chance to buy such riches. By studying textiles of the past, perhaps in books or a local museum, we can learn much about the social, economic, cultural and political life of people over the years.

KEY INVESTIGATION

Carry out an investigation into the type of clothing worn by men and women of a chosen period in the past. Make notes and sketches to show:

1. the shape of garments,
2. the types of materials used,
3. the range of colour and decoration used,
4. the accessories, such as hats and shoes, that were worn.

ANALYSIS

As a class, discuss with your teacher the influences that would have produced such styles and materials.

EVALUATION

As a class, discuss whether similar factors influence our style of dress today.

Influences on fashion

ENVIRONMENT INTERACTION

In the past, factors such as travel, war, education, social changes and the Industrial Revolution all influenced the type of clothes people wore and the type of homes they lived in. At first textiles were only produced using local raw materials such as in the woollen industry in England, the silk industry in China, and the cotton of India and North America. Dyes and patterns were all produced on a local scale and until trade began to expand, everyone had to be content with what could be produced in their own community. Once international trade began to flourish, everyone had a chance to see what was being produced elsewhere in the world, and naturally people started to desire something different. Today we have never before had so much choice or been influenced by so many different factors.

Recently communication through mass media like the cinema, TV, video, newspapers and magazines and the availability of world travel have given ordinary consumers like ourselves opportunities never before available.

It is interesting to look at modern clothes and see if we can identify what is causing their design to change so rapidly.

KEY INVESTIGATION

Look through some recent fashion magazines and cut out a number of pictures showing the influence of modern methods of communication.

ANALYSIS

Mount your illustrations and describe each in full using the following headings:
1 style,
2 type of fabric,
3 colour, texture and pattern if any,
4 cost,
5 influence of the mass media, e.g. TV serial, pop group, new films.

EVALUATION

1 Why do you think modern methods of communication are so important to changing design?
2 Which particular forms of modern communication have influenced your choice of clothes and why?

INVESTIGATION EXTENSION

Conduct a survey to find out why people in your own age group choose certain clothes.

A useful method of collecting this information is to prepare a questionnaire which covers the following points: age; sex; who or what influences your choice—friends, famous personalities, money available, magazines, TV, films, availability of shops.

Present your results in a bar chart.

VALUES

Today we are certainly lucky in that people have never before had so many consumer items to choose from. For example, if you are out shopping for a new jacket or fabric for curtains you will have hundreds of examples to choose from. Ask your parents and grandparents or any older people you know to tell you what shopping was like in their younger days. However, having so much choice can be confusing and it is important to have a good background knowledge of textiles in order to be able to make a sensible choice. This is why a knowledge of fibres and fabrics is so important. A jacket made from a poor-quality material of the wrong type may look all right in the shop but after a few weeks' wear will probably begin to look shabby. A knowledge of how colour, texture and pattern work on fabrics is vital when choosing curtain material.

Young people can make hurried purchases and then regret it. In order to minimise the danger of spending money unwisely, it is important to be aware of what the manufacturers are doing to help. In clothes, labels will give a host of information. Ready-made household textiles will also have useful labels. Fabric bought by the metre to be made up at home is only labelled on the roll so it is important to be aware of this and take note of fibre content and washing instructions when you buy it.

Labels in clothing

If you look inside any recently-purchased garments, you will often see more than one label. Most of these labels are permanent and are sewn in, but some are a 'peel off' type. Some information is to be found on swing labels too. Understanding labelling can be confusing but the information labels give is vital for making a successful purchase and helping to keep the garment in good condition.

Sewn in labels are made of fabric and are known as care labels. They are small and are to be found in seams and at the back of the neck in jumpers and jackets. They are either woven or printed with information and should be left in the garment. They should show:

- size,
- manufacturer's name,
- care instructions,
- country of origin,
- fibre content.

Sometimes this information is on two separate labels.

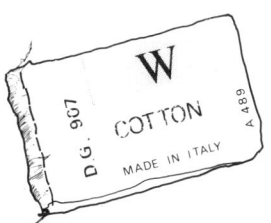

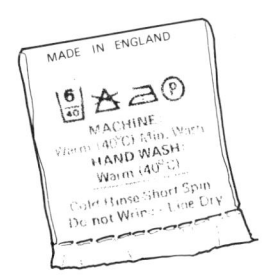

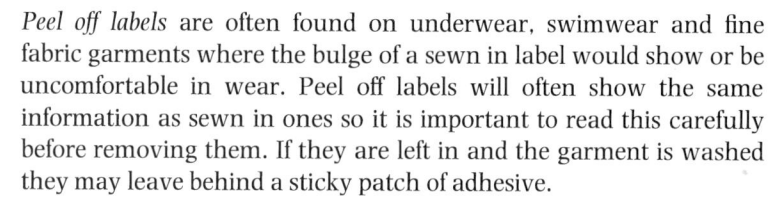

Peel off labels are often found on underwear, swimwear and fine fabric garments where the bulge of a sewn in label would show or be uncomfortable in wear. Peel off labels will often show the same information as sewn in ones so it is important to read this carefully before removing them. If they are left in and the garment is washed they may leave behind a sticky patch of adhesive.

Swing labels are usually made from card but can be plastic or even leather. They are often shaped and have a glossy finish. They may be fastened around a button or threaded through a convenient place. Obviously they are meant to be removed before the garment is worn. The information they give is usually in addition to that given on the sewn in label and will describe a particular aspect of the fabric or the maker's range of goods.

Don't forget that all textile articles should be labelled, and the information is there to help you. A sensible knitter will never choose wool without a ball band because there is so much useful information on it.

However, too often we cut out and throw away care labels because we don't realise how important they are. They are useful both when we are buying the article and afterwards. How often have you discovered, too late, that an item has to be dry cleaned? How often have you found that a jumper has come out of the washing machine several sizes smaller than it went in, or white socks have come out a delicate shade of pink? All these disasters could have been avoided if we had read the instructions given on care labels.

KEY INVESTIGATION

As a class, bring in a textile article each. Try to make sure that between you there is a selection of items to include:

casual shirt or blouse	nylon tights or stockings in unopened pack
thick winter trousers	
pleated skirt	items of underwear—male and female
hand-knitted jumper and ball band from wool used	
	pillowcase
babygro	tablecloth
quilted anorak	silky 'top'
blazer	brightly coloured towel
track suit	blanket or bedcover
sports socks (in original packing if possible)	duvet

1 Prepare a table as shown at the top of page 111.
2 Organise the items around the room so that you can circulate around them in a systematic way.
3 Examine each article and fill in the information on the table.

LABELS

Item	Number of labels	Position of label(s)	Type of label(s)	Description of label(s)	Information on label(s)
Track suit top	1	Side seam	Sewn in	Printed in two colours	Chain store name, country of origin, size, washing instructions code

▶ **ANALYSIS**

Symbol	Agitation *	Rinse *	Spinning/ Wringing *	Examples of Application
[95]	maximum	normal	normal	White cotton and linen articles without special finishes
[60]	maximum	normal	normal	Cotton, linen or viscose articles without special finishes where colours are fast at 60°C
[50]	medium	cold	short (reduced) spin	Nylon, polyester/cotton mixtures; polyester cotton and viscose articles with special finishes, cotton/acrylic mixtures
[40]	maximum	normal	normal	Cotton, linen or viscose articles, where colours are fast at 40°C but not at 60°C
[40]	medium	cold	short (reduced) spin	Acrylics, acetate and triacetate; including mixtures with wool; polyester/wool blends
[40]	minimum do not rub	normal	normal spin do not hand wring	Wool, wool mixed with other fibres; silk
(handwash symbol)	HANDWASH (DO NOT MACHINE WASH)		WASHING TEMPERATURES SHOWN IN WASH TUB SYMBOL 95 C Very Hot — Water heated to near boiling temperature. 60 C Hot — Hotter than the hand can bear. The temperature of water coming from many domestic hot taps. 50 C Hand-hot — As hot as the hand can bear. 40 C Warm — Pleasantly warm to the hand.	
⊠	DO NOT WASH			

| ⊠ DO NOT USE CHLORINE BLEACH | ◯ MAY BE TUMBLE DRIED | (iron) WARM IRON | Ⓟ DRY CLEAN ABLE |

1 Much of the important information given on care labels is in the form of symbols, numbers and letters.
   Study the International Care Labelling codes on page 111. What do the following symbols mean?

2 What does a cross drawn through a symbol mean?
3 Why is it important to be aware of *all* the information given on the labels, not just the washing instructions?
4 Select two of the articles you previously examined, sketch each and make an accurate drawing of its care label.
   Write a full description of how to care for each of the articles.

EVALUATION

1 From your investigations of a variety of articles, explain why it is so important to sort out the family wash.
2 People generally are not aware of the importance of labelling.
   Design and produce a poster which effectively brings their attention to this.

INVESTIGATION EXTENSION

1 In groups, discuss any disasters that you may have had with your washing. What were the results and how could they have been avoided?
2 If you have made a garment or textile article as part of your course, design a label to go with it.
   Include the following:
   your own exclusive 'trade' name,
   size,
   care instructions.

How can we recognise good quality in garments?

As we have seen, clear labelling should give us plenty of information about the fabric a garment is made from and how to keep it in good condition. Although checking labels is important, it is not enough to guarantee that we make a successful purchase.
   As we get to the age when we are responsible for buying our own clothes, we may well be mainly influenced by appearances only. Of

course, this is a very relevant factor, young people usually do have very strong views on what suits them, how they want to look and what they want to spend their money on. This can result, however, in some bad purchases. Clothes may be so badly made that they split at the seams, buttons may fall off and linings show.

Visual appearance (though important) is not the only criterion for choosing and buying clothes. Quality of materials and workmanship are also important factors in purchasing clothes that are value for money. How can we judge quality? Let's look at a particular garment—a shirt. This is a common article of clothing worn by both sexes, by young and old and for casual or more formal wear.

Firstly, look at the fabric itself. This is often made from a mixture of man-made and natural fibres such as polyester/cotton, but may be entirely of man-made or natural fibres. Shirt fabric is usually lightweight and of a close woven structure, although there are shirts of heavier fabrics and those of a knitted type. The fabric may be plain or patterned, colours will vary from white to strong colours. The style may be classic, with long sleeves and a stiffened collar or be more casually styled. Whatever the type of shirt, it will have been made from a number of individual pieces of fabric, cut and sewn together to give a finished style and shape to the garment.

The performance of the fabric itself will depend on the factors mentioned above, its fibre content and method of construction. Most shirts are made from fair- to good-quality materials so it is in the making up of the garment that the consumer will mostly notice differences. Shops and stores carry out their own tests on new products to determine their quality. For textiles these are extensive and range from testing for colour fastness and the strength of the seams to sizes of buttons and buttonholes.

For the average consumer a thorough visual check when buying clothes is important. Do not be afraid to look inside the garment, study the label and compare prices.

Sometimes we only want a garment to last a short time, then we will probably buy a 'high fashion' article and not be too worried about its quality. On the other hand, goods must be fit for their purpose (see page 125) and should not fall below a certain standard. As people get older, they are generally prepared to pay more for their clothes and be guaranteed a better-quality and longer-lasting product. Most of us, though, need clothes that are a balance between short-life 'high fashion' and long-life 'classics'.

To sum up, a good-quality garment should be made well and from an attractive hard-wearing fabric, it should fit well, be fashionable yet functional, have and keep its good appearance and enhance the manufacturer's good name.

These rules can be said to be the 'criteria' by which we judge the quality of a garment. We should expect all the clothes we buy to conform to this basic means of judging good quality. Do not be afraid to look thoroughly for these points.

The following tables will help you identify the features of garments where you should expect to find good quality.

Some of these features will also apply to items for household and other uses, such as sports kit, bedlinen, etc.

Criteria for assessing materials used in garments

Fabric	1 Should be suitable for the type of garment and its style. 2 Should be suitable in weight and texture. 3 Should have no flaws. 4 Should be correctly printed or woven.
Thread	1 Should be a suitable match for the fabric—colour and fibre type. 2 Avoid transparent thread.
Lining	Garment may be fully or part lined. See under **Fabric**.
Trimming or decoration	1 Should be suitable for garment type and style. 2 Should be compatible with garment fabric regarding washing, ironing, drying. 3 Should enhance garment.

Fastenings	Zips: 1 Correct colour, type, weight.
	      2 Should have suitable method of application.
	
	Buttons: 1 Well-chosen for colour, style, size, shape.
	         2 Should be strongly sewn on.
	
	Buttonholes: 1 Should be correct size for buttons.
	             2 Should be in correct positions.
	             3 Should be strong especially at ends.
	
	Other fastenings: (velcro, press studs, hooks and eyes)
	             1 Should be correct type and size.
	             2 Should be in correct position.
	             3 Should be well secured.

Belt	1 Should be suitable in size. 2 Should be suitable in style. 3 Should have matching coloured eyelets. 4 Should be compatible with garment regarding washing, ironing, etc. (or be separately labelled). 5 Should have strong carriers correctly positioned.

Criteria for assessing the quality of workmanship in clothing

Stitches	1 Should be correct type for fabric. 2 Should be uniform in size. 3 Should be well secured at ends.
Seams	1 Should be flat on outside of garment with no puckering. 2 Should be of even width. 3 Seam allowance should be generous not skimped. 4 Should be neatened. 5 Should be suitable type for fabric used and garment style.
Hems	1 Should be suitable type for fabric and style of garment. 2 Should be inconspicuous on right side. 3 Should be suitable in depth. 4 Should have well-pressed lower edge, smooth not wavy.
Openings	1 Should be suitable type for garment style. 2 Should be adequate length. 3 Should be strong particularly at end where most strain occurs.
Darts	1 Should be correct length. 2 Should be in correct position. 3 Should be well pressed.
Pockets	Can be functional or for decoration only 1 If functional, should be in correct position. 2 Should be strongly made and possibly lined.
Collars	1 Should be set on evenly and centrally. 2 Under collar should not show. 3 Should be comfortable.
Sleeves	1 Should hang correctly. 2 Should be of correct length and width. 3 Should be comfortable with enough ease to move, i.e. not too tight. 4 Should have well-neatened armhole.
Skirt or trouser legs	1 Should hang correctly. 2 Should be comfortable. 3 Should have level hem.
Label	Should have care labels securely attached in sensible position.

KEY INVESTIGATION

Bring in a favourite garment which you have recently bought. Examine it carefully, inside and out and discuss your findings with other members of your group.

CONSUMER AWARENESS

▷ **ANALYSIS**

1 Using headings: fabric, thread, fastenings and include trimming or decoration, lining and belt if your garment has these, analyse each and enter a tick in the column which you feel best expresses the quality.

Quality	Excellent	Good	Fair	Poor
Fabric Thread Lining Trimming/ Decoration Fastenings Belt				

2 Look at your garment in more detail and analyse the quality of the processes used in its making.

Record your results on a table. Omit any processes that are not present in your garment.

	Comment
Stitches	
Seams	
Hems	
Openings	
Darts	
Pockets	
Collar	
Sleeves	
Skirt or trouser leg	
Label	

EVALUATION

1. Do you consider that the materials used in your garment are generally,
   Excellent, Good, Fair or Poor?
2. Do you consider that the processes used to construct your garment are generally,
   Excellent, Good, Fair or Poor?
3. Is your garment deteriorating with wear? What are its strong points? What are its weak points?
4. How much did you pay for your garment? Do you consider this a fair price?

INVESTIGATION EXTENSION

If you have recently made a garment or textile article, evaluate it in relation to what you have learned during the previous exercise.

Let's keep our clothes in good condition

It is obviously very important to keep our clothes clean and to regularly change sheets, wash or dry clean curtains, carpets, cushions, lampshades and other household textiles. In times past, women did all the washing and ironing on one day of the week,

Laundry equipment from 1947

CONSUMER AWARENESS

EFFICIENCY

HEALTH

usually Monday. Soap was grated beforehand and textiles were boiled up in 'coppers', pounded with sticks or 'dollies' and whites were treated to a 'blue bag' and starch. Ask your grandmother or elderly friends about washdays. Washing used to be very hard work but in addition, laundry had to be put through a wringer to squeeze out the water, then hung out to dry in the garden or yard. Often, clean washing was covered in smuts from factory chimneys or passing steam trains. Ironing was a back breaking job too. Flat irons were heated on the fire on a special trivet or on top of the kitchen range. They then had to be carried to the table to be used. Sheets were smoothed flat by being put through a mangle.

Most fabrics in the past were made from natural fibres and so could stand the heat of the boiling water and the iron without damage.

Today we take for granted the equipment available to us. Make a list of all the labour-saving laundry equipment you have at home and assess the time taken in actually handling the washing. Even if you don't have a washing machine at home, there is usually a launderette nearby. Most homes have an electric iron these days and some have tumble dryers. Most homes also have airing cupboards where textiles can be thoroughly aired after ironing and before use.

Modern laundry equipment

With all these modern aids to save us time and long, hard work, it is still necessary for us to make a personal effort to keep our clothing looking good.

Modern fabrics, if washed and pressed regularly, should keep their bright, fresh appearance. Much of our clothing these days is for casual and informal wear but there are still occasions when our outfits need to be crisp, well pressed and in 'tip top' condition.

KEEPING CLOTHES IN GOOD CONDITION

VALUES

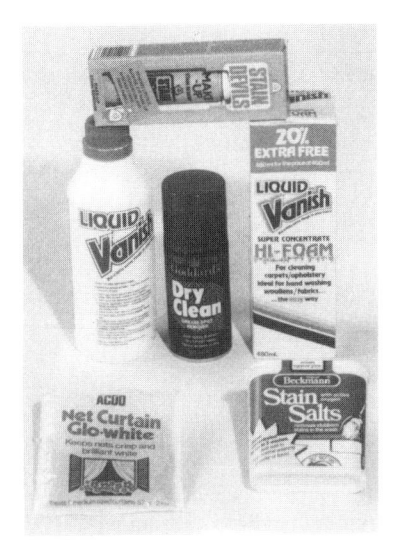

We all need to take responsibility for our own possessions and we should take pride in looking after our shoes and clothes. These should never be put away dirty or stained. Put 'out of season' clothes away carefully, clean, pressed and folded. Quite often stains are difficult to remove if they are not treated at once. There are many preparations in the shops today which will remove stubborn stains and grease marks. Stains will usually come out if they are treated straight away by soaking in cold water. Loose dust and dirt can easily be removed by brushing.

Stain removers

Common stains

From time to time, accidents happen and stains can occur on our clothes, bedlinen, towels and other textile articles. These stains can be put into three main groups:

GREASE   PROTEIN   ACID

Grease stains could be from cooking fat (chips) or perhaps from make-up.
Protein stains could be from milk, blood, egg.
Acid stains could be from fruit juice.

KEY INVESTIGATION

1. In groups make a list of the common stains that you have all noticed on textile articles.
2. Stains can usually be put in one of three groups. Grease, protein or acid. Put the stains you have listed into the three groups.
3. Using the reference material your teacher will have provided, find out how such stains may be removed.
4. Carry out some simple tests on pieces of cotton fabric, polyester fabric and a wool-mix fabric.
    a. Take each fabric in turn and put common stains such as lipstick, blood, ink, tea, paint and fruit juice on each.
    b. Cut each stained fabric into three pieces. Label each section and keep a note of the stain used.
    c. For each fabric, keep one section as a control, soak the second in cold water and wash the third piece in hot water and washing powder.
       You may like to try different types of washing powder and note the results.
    d. Make a table on which to record your results.
    e. If any stains remain, refer to the resource material that your teacher provided to find a suitable method of removal.
       Record your results.

5 Commercial stain removal products are quite expensive. Check prices and availability in the shops and ask your local dry cleaning shop how they treat stains.

▷ ANALYSIS

Referring to the results of your investigation, what is the best action to take when:
a a young child spills milk over its clothes?
b you cut your finger in the kitchen and get blood on your shirt?
c playing a sport, you get grass stains on your shorts?
d you sit on a piece of chewing gum in a café?

☐ EVALUATION

Do you think it is wise to attempt to tackle stain removal at home or should you leave it to the experts? Give opinions on both sides of the argument.

LET'S LOOK AT SHOPS AND SHOPPING

HUMAN DEVELOPMENT

From an early age, we begin to take an interest in clothes and have strong views about what we want to wear. Parents generally feel that it is better to pay for clothes that their children choose rather than to buy what they think they would like. Otherwise the clothes would be little worn and turn out to be a waste of money. It is only in recent years that children and young people have had the kind of choice that we have today. In the distant past, children were dressed as miniature adults with no regard for their need to play and move freely in their clothes. In the more recent past, probably up until the 1950s, parents chose clothes for their children and kept them in rather 'babyish' clothes until their early teens.

VALUES

Today, however, children and young people often have their own pocket or birthday money to spend, they might have a Saturday or holiday job and are able to purchase their own clothing and sometimes even the textiles used in their own rooms. Designers today have a clear idea of what young consumers want and work hard to meet the demands. There are many shops these days, like *Top Shop*, selling clothing aimed at the younger age groups. In our larger stores, there are large sections devoted to these age groups.

In addition to shops, there are a number of other ways of buying clothes, accessories and household textiles. It is usual for young consumers to identify the kind of clothes that suit them and the places where they can buy such clothes. It may be that you like the

SHOPS AND SHOPPING

styles and colours sold in one shop, would buy your shoes in another but would buy an outfit for a special occasion somewhere else. Most of us spend quite a lot of time window shopping, looking through magazines and catalogues and swapping ideas with friends. By doing this, we are storing up ideas and developing our own 'taste' so that when we have the means to buy, we can make a satisfactory purchase.

KEY INVESTIGATION

In groups, carry out a survey of your neighbourhood, or nearest town if you live in a rural area, to find out where clothing can be bought.

Make a table of your findings.

Name of shop/stall	Type of shop/market	Age group catered for	Price range (high, medium, low)	Choice
Marks & Spencer	Large chain store	All ages	High to medium	Quite good

ANALYSIS

From your findings,
1. describe the provision for buying clothes in your area. What type of shop is missing that you would find useful?
2. How many shops sold both clothing and household textiles? Is this helpful?
3. How influenced are you by:
   a displays
   b shop layout
   c shop staff

121

☐ EVALUATION

Write a full description of the type of clothing shop you would like to see in your neighbourhood. How does this compare with the provision that you have found locally?

Alternative methods of shopping

Apart from different kinds of shops, chain stores, shops within shops, specialist shops and markets, many people find it convenient to do 'armchair' shopping. Of course, for many people, this is the only way they can shop. They may be disabled, housebound or live in a remote part of the country. For the ordinary shopper, it is often more convenient to use mail order too as time available for shopping may be limited and the heat and crush of Saturday shopping unbearable to some.

Mail order shopping started in the 1920s in the North of England and the Midlands and at first was aimed at working class people who found they couldn't afford to pay for goods outright. The catalogues offered all items of household use including clothes. Agents would come round and collect the payment in instalments. These catalogues were thick, heavy volumes and all orders were received and delivered by post. This method of shopping became widespread and reached its peak in the 1970s. There are few of us who haven't seen a catalogue from companies like *Littlewoods, Grattan, Freemans, Empire* and *Great Universal Stores*.

Why are these heavy catalogues now going out of use? This may be for two reasons. One is that credit selling is now available in all the High Street shops and the other is that the goods in catalogues could not compete with the new image of many of the up and coming chain stores which were enjoying a complete refit. Today, however, mail order shopping is again on the increase but the new catalogues for clothes are quite different from the earlier ones.

We can either send off for these or buy these direct from our High Street shops. The goods on sale through these 'new look' catalogues show exclusive collections of co-ordinated ranges. *Warehouse*'s 'Bymail' was one of the first of these. They are aimed at a much younger consumer than the earlier general catalogues, often have large pages but are thinner and have really good photographs of clothes and accessories being worn by top models photographed on location. Distributors like *Freemans* and *Grattan* are now producing their own 'slimmer' and more specialist catalogues. There are some excellent ones which specialise in children's clothing. Now, there is even telephone ordering, which was introduced by *Freemans*, *Empire Stores* and *Littlewoods* in the 1980s.

KEY INVESTIGATION

Your teacher will give you addresses of mail order organisations to send for catalogues or you can send off for some which you will see advertised in magazines and newspapers.

As a group, try to acquire as many different types of catalogues as possible.

Individually, decide on an article of your choice, e.g. a sweatshirt, and price such an article in local shops. Look for this article in the catalogues when they are available and compare prices.

▷ ANALYSIS

When the catalogues arrive, analyse the information they contain and record this on a table such as the one below.

Catalogue	Types of goods	Age range	Price range	Choice
Penny Plain	Knitted jumpers, cardigans	Teens to forties	Expensive	Small but exclusive

EVALUATION

From your study of a variety of catalogues and the goods they offer for sale, answer the following:
1 Which particular groups of the public would find this method of shopping most useful and why?
2 How do the prices of mail order goods compare with those bought locally?
3 In your opinion, what would be the main advantages and disadvantages of mail order shopping to someone in your own age group?

Methods of payment

When we go to the shops with a particular purchase in mind it is necessary to decide beforehand how we will pay for the goods.

In the past, most people were paid each week in cash therefore the method of payment for goods tended to be by cash. Sometimes an expensive item was paid for week by week in a method known as hire purchase. These days, many people are paid by cheque or are worried about carrying large sums of money about in a busy shopping centre. In addition, shops offer customers opportunities to pay by charge card; *Marks & Spencer, John Lewis Partnership* shops and many High Street shops offer this system of payment to customers.

In some areas, whole towns have their own charge card system so that consumers need carry only one card which enables them to shop for anything in the town. They can be used in supermarkets and garages as well as in more specialised shops.

Credit cards like *Visa* and *Access* are another common method of payment, due to their increased availability and popularity.

KEY INVESTIGATION

Find out how many methods of payment there are available today which people use for the purchase of clothes and household textiles. Produce a questionnaire which will help you gather this information and when you have recorded your results, answer the following questions.

ANALYSIS

1 What is the most popular method of payment for clothes?
2 How do people pay for larger items of household textiles, for instance, carpets?
3 How popular have you found charge cards to be?
4 What percentage of people did you find still pay by cash or cheque?

EVALUATION

1 What are the main reasons for the popularity of non-cash payments?
2 Do you think there are any disadvantages in not paying for goods directly, i.e. by cash or cheque?

Let's look at consumers' rights

Have you ever bought a garment which split at the seams, which had a broken zip or a bad flaw in the fabric? If so, what did you do about it? If you did nothing because you thought it was a waste of time, then you were mistaken. The law now is very clear. If the goods do not conform to the following rules, then you have the right to demand a complete refund, or accept the faulty goods and receive a certain amount of refund, or get a complete replacement or free repair.

The three rules laid down by the Sale of Goods Act 1979 are:
1 Goods must be of merchantable quality, this means, they must be fit for their purpose, must not be damaged or broken.
2 Goods must be as described on the package or in the display, or as described by the seller.
3 Goods must be fit for their particular purpose.

If things do go wrong with what you have bought, you must take action as soon as possible. Make a complaint by taking the article back to the shop, by phoning or by writing. Whichever action you take it will help if you have the receipt or proof of purchase, ask for the manager or shop owner and do *not* lose your temper.

If you have received something as a present and it proves faulty, it is the buyer who should deal with it, not you.

KEY INVESTIGATION

Your teacher will provide you with some information from the Office of Fair Trading, published by HMSO. Read through the booklets.

ANALYSIS

Answer the following questions.
1 You have just bought a new cotton sweatshirt. When you get it home, you discover the welt is pulling away—the stitches have come undone. What would you do? What should the shop do?
2 You buy a jacket in a sale and discover when you try it on at home that a pocket lining is torn. On taking it back to the shop, you see a notice saying 'No Refunds'. What would you do?

☐ EVALUATION

From your investigations you will have identified basic consumer rights. Design a poster, to go on either a school notice board or in some other prominent position, which informs people of these rights.

INVESTIGATION EXTENSION

1 Find out all you can about consumer groups in your area. How are these operating and what help do they offer the consumer?
2 Find out what the role of your local Trading Standards Department is and how it can help the consumer.

Let's look at advertising

We are all used to being bombarded with advertising—on TV, radio, through magazines and newspapers and of course through posters, large and small. These forms of advertising are visually and aurally attractive. Often we find it difficult to ignore them. Large-scale posters in prominent public places or catchy tunes played repeatedly on TV constantly catch our eye or ear.

Advertising, particularly that aimed at young people, is cleverly designed to make you feel that you can't do without the product, whatever it may be. This form of advertising usually works on a visual level only, notice how few words are needed to explain the product. There is an old saying 'pictures speak louder than words': this is particularly true of much fashion advertising.

The designers of such material—posters, leaflets, magazine advertisements and so on—work from a brief. Designers may work for an advertising company or work free lance; that is, they work independently and are engaged for particular jobs. We will look at one way in which fashion advertising operates.

The brief may be very precise or be quite broad, it may be to advertise a complete collection of clothes or just one single item. The creative ability of the designer or design team is put into top gear when a new assignment is given. As you will already know, the fashion world plans far ahead of the time the clothes actually appear in the shops. Once the clothes are made up, designers and photographers get to work.

Designers use all the design elements to create the advertisements that will show the clothes off to the best advantage. Elements of form, colour, texture, line, pattern, space and light are put together to form pictures of instant visual appeal.

One of the important decisions that have to be made early on is to identify the potential customers for the garments that will be shown. This group of customers is called the target group. It would be no good producing pictures that would appeal to the middle aged if the garments were aimed at the teenage market. Carry out the investigation and you will discover how visual impact is achieved in advertising.

KEY INVESTIGATION

As a group, bring some up-to-date fashion magazines or leaflets in to school. Look through these and select two different advertisements each. Cut these out and display them on a suitable board in the classroom.

ANALYSIS

1. As a group, discuss the main design features that you feel have been used to promote the garments to advantage. Produce a table so that these features can be recorded. An example is shown overleaf but you may wish to include features other than these.

Subject of advertisement	Source	Target audience	Colours	Background	Accessories
Lycra swimwear	Look-in magazine	Teens	Bright primaries	Beach scene, West Indies	Shells, hammock

2   Label each of the advertisements in the display, and carry out a survey which asks as many pupils as possible which three advertisements they feel are the most effective. Devise a method of recording this information.

EVALUATION

Looking at the results of your survey and the table recording design features, can you identify the factors that make an effective advertisement?

INVESTIGATION EXTENSION

Individually, select an item of clothing that is a firm favourite of yours, and, imagining that you are the manufacturer of that garment, design an advertisement for it to be published in a popular magazine.

How reliable are advertisements?

Of course, all manufacturers will be doing their best to make the advertisements for their goods eye-catching and striking. There is a great deal of competition in the clothing industry and an enormous amount of money is spent on advertising. If you remember, in Section 3 when we looked at the beginning of the design process, we discovered that a lot of time, effort and money is put in over a period of years to develop the product. This being the case, the product must be presented to the public in an imaginative and attractive way.

However, there has to be a safeguard to ensure that no false claims for the product are made.

Under the Trade Descriptions Act 1968, a misleading advertisement is an offence. If there is any complaint to be made, we can report it to our local Trading Standards Department. In the case of difficulty, the complaint can be taken direct to the Advertising Standards Authority (ASA). Complaints about advertising on TV, cable and radio can be dealt with by the Independent Broadcasting Authority (IBA) or the Cable Authority.

5

Technology in Clothing and Textiles

TECHNOLOGY IN CLOTHING AND TEXTILES

New technology has made a great impact on all aspects of textiles, both in industry and on a domestic level. In school you may have had the opportunity to use a computerised sewing machine or to try out some designs on a computer using one of the new software programs. However, it is in the textile and garment industries that most developments and changes have been, and are continuing to be, made.

LET'S LOOK AT RECENT CHANGES IN THE PRODUCTION OF TEXTILES

In Section 2, we looked at some of the interesting yarns that are available for the making of both woven and knitted textiles. Some of the most interesting and useful technological changes have been in the production of new machines that can make these fancy yarns. One method now widely used is known as 'hollow spindle' spinning. The equipment used enables the manufacturers to produce some of the most beautifully soft yet textured yarns. Here is a diagram to help you understand how it works.

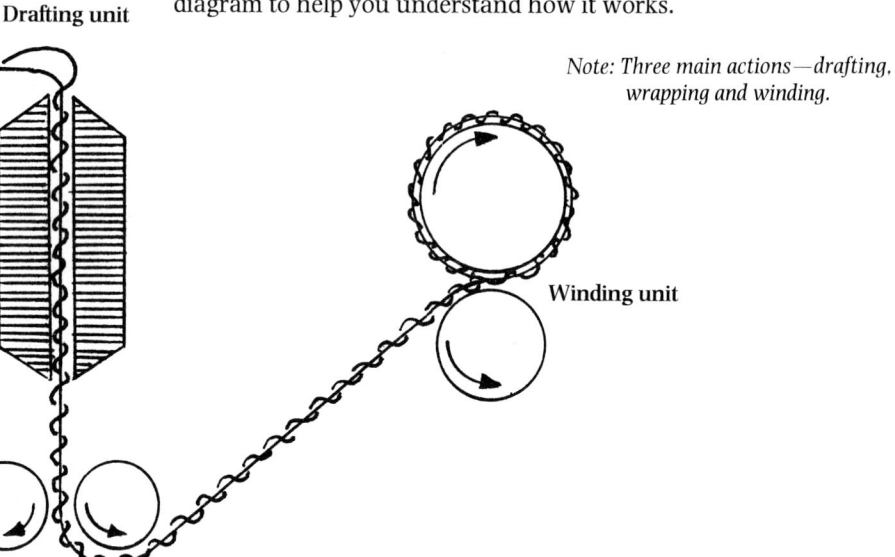

Note: Three main actions—drafting, wrapping and winding.

- Sliver, roving or yarn
- Rollers
- Drafting unit
- Binder yarn
- Hollow spindle unit with bobbin of binder
- Rotates and wraps yarn
- Rollers
- Winding unit

Hollow spindle spinning

The yarns produced by this method all have one characteristic in common. They are 'wrapped' by a binder which holds all the loose fibres together.

In addition to this, much fancy yarn is now produced on a fancy twisting machine, which can be entirely computerised. You have already looked at the basic method of putting a twist into yarns so will not be surprised to know that this process can now be done much faster, with more variations and virtually at the touch of a button. This diagram will help you to understand the principles behind this process.

CHANGES IN TEXTILE PRODUCTION

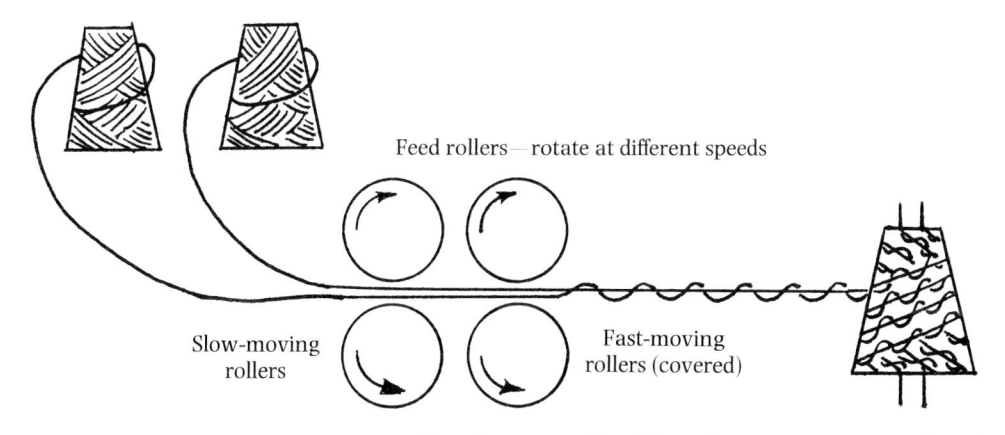

Fancy twisting machinery

Feed rollers — rotate at different speeds

Slow-moving rollers

Fast-moving rollers (covered)

Note: By the use of fast/slow rollers, some yarns come through straight, others come through loose and wrapped around

AESTHETICS
EFFICIENCY

At the touch of a button, the operator can control the flow of supply yarns into the machine and by varying the speed at which the rollers rotate, can change the yarn's appearance. This process means that short 'runs' of yarns can be produced quickly and cheaply and the manufacturer can respond to the customers' needs which in turn must meet the demand from shop buyers and consumers for up-to-date colours and textures. The biggest problem is in the initial investment in the equipment, which is very expensive. The yarn designer and machine operator must work closely together to ensure the yarn produced has an outlet.

TECHNOLOGY

Obviously, if new technology has a part to play in the production of yarns, then it must also feature in the manufacture of fabrics. In knitted, woven and printed textiles, computerisation is playing an increasingly important part. CAD (computer aided design) is being used to develop new fabrics quickly and accurately to meet the needs of clothing and textile industry. CAD enables the operator to produce on the VDU (visual display unit) possible designs in full colour.

Such designs can be built up using a keyboard, stylus or 'mouse'. Taking a single unit of design which might be made up of lines and solid areas, the positions of these are plotted by the operator and will be shown on the screen. Colour schemes can be tried out, the scale changed and repeats produced until the operator is satisfied with the result. This can then be stored in the computer or printed out in colour. These full-colour prints are very useful in that the designer can see at a glance what the design will really look like. For instance, if it is for carpeting, the paper print out can be laid on the floor to get a realistic idea of how the design will work. If it is for curtaining, then the print out can be put up vertically and even pleated to get a good idea of the finished result.

Once the design has been judged to be suitable, it can be transferred to the appropriate machine for manufacture. This might be on a circular knitting machine, or a loom. The computer can also relay the design information directly to a fabric printing area where screens are produced photographically for each of the colours to be used.

As you will have seen, all these new processes have done much to shorten the time from the initial design idea to the finished length of fabric.

New technology in the garment industry

In Section 2 pages 80–1, there is a flow chart showing the stages in the design and manufacture of garments. You will have noticed the word COMPUTER occurring a number of times in the right-hand column. Study the flow chart as you read this section. Modern technology has helped to transform a declining industry into a competitive and profitable one. As you will know, the British textile industry has suffered over recent years from the import of cheap and well-made clothes from countries of the Far East. In order to compete with such a strong market, particularly the cheap labour costs, the British manufacturers have had to change production methods and develop the technology to improve the quality of their goods and to speed up the time taken to get the goods into the shops. This is the reason modern technology is now so important and why the factories making clothes today employ so few people compared with the past.

The use of the computer in garment design

EFFICIENCY

The traditional image of the dress designer sketching ideas for the new collection still exists, but many designers today take advantage of technology to help them create and visualise their ideas. CAD and computer graphics now allow the designer to create the image on a screen and to superimpose fabric designs and colours on it. A three-dimensional image is also possible so that the designer can view the design from all sides, which is an extremely lengthy process if it has to be done by sketching front, side and back views. The next step will be to produce an animated image on screen which will imitate the models showing off the clothes on a catwalk!

Pattern making and grading

Some of the most time- and labour-saving operations in garment manufacture take place during the pattern design and grading stages. This is the stage where the design is translated into pattern pieces from basic blocks. Computer software has now been developed to allow this to be done on a screen. The basic shapes are stored in the computer and the operator uses a stylus or 'mouse' to make

NEW TECHNOLOGY

Computer aided design

alterations to those shapes until the desired effects are produced. Having been designed in one size, the pattern pieces are then graded, by computer, to the number of different sizes required.

Lay planning and cutting out

As you know if you have cut out and made an article from a commercial paper pattern, the placing of the paper pieces correctly on the fabric is an important task. Industrially, the task is much more important. It is essential that the fabric is cut economically with as little waste as possible. Waste fabric means loss of profit so must be kept to a minimum. This is where the computer comes in. The graded pattern pieces are stored in the memory and may be displayed on a screen on an area corresponding to the width of the fabric to be used. The pieces may be moved around, rotated or reversed until the most economical 'lay plan' is found. The computer can do this automatically and will work out the amount of waste and then cost the fabric required for each garment.

If your previous experience includes using a paper pattern, you will know that once the pieces are correctly pinned on to the fabric they then have to be cut out. In your case, you will cut out only one or two pieces from each pattern piece, through either single or double fabric. On an industrial level, fabric is layered on to a cutting table, sometimes interleaved with paper depending on the number of garments ordered.

EFFICIENCY

It may be necessary to cut hundreds or even thousands of pieces out from the same pattern. Computer-controlled cutting has made this operation quicker, more accurate and safer. Pieces can be cut

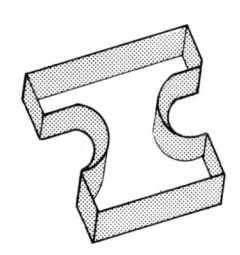

Die for cutting out briefs

out using a knife, a laser or a jet of water! Because the computer memory has been able to store the shapes of the pattern pieces, this information can be relayed direct to the cutting tool. This is an expensive procedure but much faster and more accurate than manually operated machines. Laser cutting creates heat along the cutting edge and may fuse multiple layers of fabric together so it can only be used for a low number of plies; the computer-controlled knife is the most efficient cutter of many layers of fabric. Some small sections of garments and small knitted articles such as underwear are often cut out using 'dies'. These are like pastry cutters, metal shapes made to exact requirements, which are then pressed through the layers of fabric, cutting as they go.

Garment assembly

CAM (computer aided manufacture) is now recognised as being essential to the smooth and speedy making-up process. Garments can be made up in one of two different ways and we will look at each of these in turn.

The first method is the one you will be familiar with, this is called the 'make through' system. Here, each machinist is highly skilled and can perform all the sewing processes needed to complete the garment. The machinist receives all the cut out pieces necessary for each garment and works alone to produce the finished article. This is a slow process and output is low.

The second method is known as 'sectionalisation'. This system involves each machinist carrying out only one operation, then the work is passed to the next person, and so on until the garment is complete. Because each machinist or operator does only one job, the rate of production is much quicker. Unfortunately, the machinist, who may be sewing something like collars all day, can get very bored and enjoys very little job satisfaction, never actually seeing a complete garment. The 'make through' system offers the worker more individual control and the satisfaction of seeing the garment complete. 'Sectionalisation' is very complex and requires the work to flow smoothly and evenly through the factory. The organisation and planning of this requires a high level of production management. In order to reduce the time machinists have to handle their particular component, various systems have been developed to pass the work around the factory. A computer will control the overhead transporter system so that components are fed around the machinists at a pace which enables them to carry out their job efficiently. You can imagine what it must be like sitting at a machine with your work piling up! Machinists working on this system are generally paid at 'piece work' rates according to various factors including their efficiency, the degree of difficulty of the operation and the time taken to carry out the work. Obviously, it is in their interests to work quickly and accurately, thus producing the most work in the least time. The sewing machines being developed today are able auto-

VALUES

EFFICIENCY

matically to carry out the individual processes which, at one time, skilled machinists would have done. Operators now have only to feed the components into the machine and the sewing process will be done automatically. Sewing on buttons and making buttonholes is a process which is now done in this way but is only one example of many. It is beginning to look as if the days of the skilled worker in the garment industry are numbered.

Pressing and finishing

You will know how important it is to press seams and darts as you make up a garment and to give it a good final press. A dry or steam iron would be used to get the best result on the particular fabric you are using. In industry, pressing and steaming machines are used on different parts of the garments and microprocessor control enables the different fabrics and types of garments to be finished off to look their best. You may have seen slightly less sophisticated machines being used at your local dry cleaning shop.

KEY INVESTIGATION

If your teacher can arrange for you to have a visit to a nearby garment manufacturer, you will be able to carry out this investigation.
1. As a group, make a list of the points that you will be looking for during the visit.
2. You may not be able to make notes whilst you are in the factory but afterwards discuss what you have seen and write a short report.

ANALYSIS

1. What type(s) of garments were being made at the factory?
2. How many operations did you see being carried out?
3. How many people are employed at the factory and how are they occupied?
4. What kind of training did they undergo?
5. How much of the work was automated and how much manual?
6. Were computers used at any stage of the operations?

EVALUATION

1. How important do you think modern technology was in the making of the garments you saw on your visit?
2. In what ways might this be further developed and what might be the consequence of this?

INVESTIGATION EXTENSION

EFFICIENCY

Visit a local dressmaker or bespoke tailor and find out how he/she obtains work and carries it out. Compare this with what you witnessed on your factory visit if you made one.

LET'S LOOK AT TECHNOLOGY AND THE CONSUMER

As consumers, there are many ways in which our purchases of garments and other household textiles are associated with new technology. Most shops and stores these days have their stock controlled by computer and of course, payment made by either cash or personal cheque at the till or by cash card or credit card is recorded using new technology. An interesting and useful asset to the person who does his/her sewing at home is a recent service which entails making a basic pattern to fit your individual measurements. A computer will store these dimensions and any changes that might occur in your size can be made in seconds! In future, the problem of spending time selecting patterns from catalogues and waiting only to find the shop is out of your size will not exist. Indeed, shops will not hold stocks of patterns as at present. As a customer, you will be able to advise the pattern service of your needs, and the computer operator, having access to your stored measurements, will be able to make the exact pattern available to you.

In the future, it is possible to foresee that shopping as we know it will disappear! Already there are services available, known as fashion consultancies, which use a computer to record their customers' measurements, likes and dislikes, colour preferences and available amounts of money to spend on clothes. The customer has only to pick up the phone and tell the consultant that a particular type of garment is required for a particular occasion, and the computer, linked to all the major designers, stores and boutiques, will find out where the best buy for that customer is to be found. Another phone call and the garment can be delivered to the customer's home. Of course, this is an expensive way to shop as the initial fee is quite high, but for men and women who run businesses or have other demanding careers, it can be a great time and money saver in the long run.

EFFICIENCY

For the rest of us, the developing idea of telephone-order shopping is more likely to be used. Technology is being used in this way to reach customers more efficiently but also to ensure that the goods on offer are what they want. In the future, with the spread of cable television, it is possible that we will be able to do our shopping from home by ordering goods through television. In the United States home shopping television programmes are all the rage! The future looks set for us to have displays of new fashions on our television

Computer sewing

You may have computerised sewing machines in school, at home or possibly you've seen them demonstrated by a local supplier. These new machines are quite different from the more conventional straight stitch or even the fully automatic machines that you have probably used. The greatest differences lie in the mechanisms. The earlier machines needed many hundreds of working parts to enable the machine to sew the variety of stitches needed. Computer machines have replaced the cams that produced the stitches with a 'chip'—a microprocessor and a memory bank. You may have seen a sewing-machine mechanic servicing a conventional machine in school. This is a long and messy job demanding skills which are not necessary with the new machines. If a computerised machine does develop a fault, then the mechanic can plug in an instrument which will diagnose where the fault lies. The faulty part can be quickly removed and replaced with a new one, thus making the job of repair cheaper and less messy. The machine also looks different. If you can, place a conventional zigzag machine next to a computerised machine and compare the two. There may not be much difference in size and overall shape but you will notice the greatest changes in the controls.

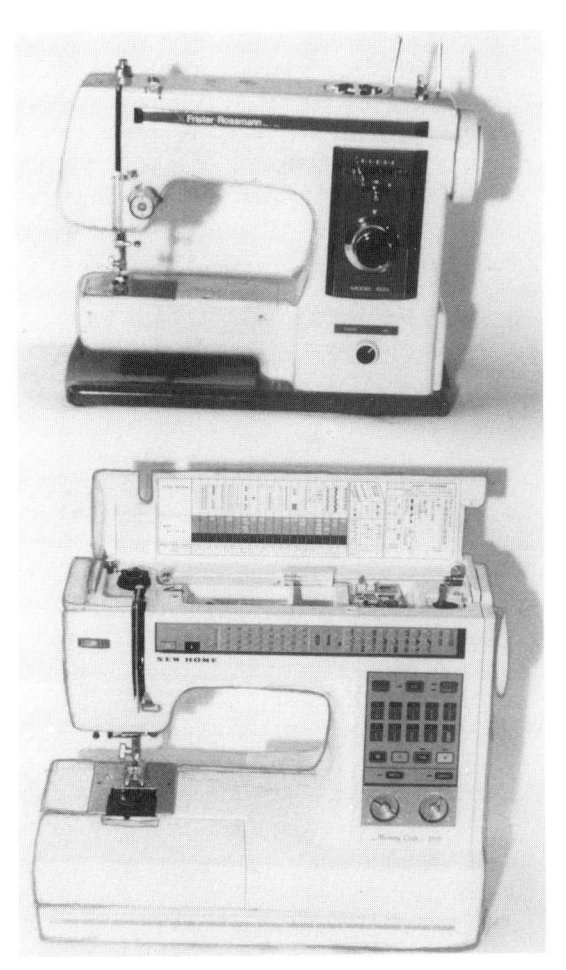

Conventional (top) and computerised (bottom) sewing machines

EFFICIENCY

On the older type of machine, you will notice that changes in stitch length and needle swing are obtained by adjusting a number of different levers and buttons. This is something that is often difficult to do, you may remember having problems getting stitches just right! With the new types of machine, there are no levers to move or buttons to turn. The controls are underneath the 'touch' panels and only light finger pressure is needed to change the stitch. These machines will always give exact and perfect results every time using the memory. The struggles that you previously had in getting good results will be a thing of the past. Computerised machines are very easy to use and to understand. They can be used by very young

HEALTH

children and by people suffering from disability caused by a disease like arthritis, even the severely disabled and handicapped can use these machines. The other advantages concern the machine's ability to perform well on a variety of modern fabrics. Stitches have been developed to sew everything from fine, silky polyester jerseys, to denim and leather. In addition, the decorative stitches, figures and letters of the alphabet can be used in any chosen sequence to create

AESTHETICS

delightful and personal touches.

KEY INVESTIGATION

Try this simple experiment on a computerised machine.
1. Take a small piece of plain cotton fabric, approximately 8 cm × 10 cm and iron a piece of Vilene on the back. Then using either felt pens or fabric dye pens, draw a few simple curved lines on it. Make a simple pattern by overlapping the curved lines.
2. Thread up the machine with a strong-coloured thread.
3. Select a decorative stitch and work it over the drawn lines using the reverse feed to go over the area several times.
4. Change to another colour, select another stitch and do the same again over another set of lines.
5. Carry on until you have a well-balanced design of lines and textured fillings.
6. You may add a few hand-worked stitches, beads, or some individual initials worked on the machine.

ANALYSIS

Rate the following activities on a scale of 1 to 4 (1 = low, 4 = high). Copy the list into your books and ring the appropriate number.

1. Preparation for sewing:
Threading up	1	2	3	4
Winding the bobbin	1	2	3	4
Selection of stitch	1	2	3	4

2   Stitching:

Quality of stitches (even tension)	1	2	3	4
Reverse sewing	1	2	3	4
Changing stitches	1	2	3	4

3   Design aspects:

Appearance of stitches	1	2	3	4
Textural effects	1	2	3	4
Colour thread change	1	2	3	4

EVALUATION

Write a short article for your school magazine which describes the advantages of using a computerised machine and encourages other pupils to try their hand at using one.

INVESTIGATION EXTENSION

1   Design a personal logo to include your name and some additional decoration. Work the logo on felt using different-coloured backgrounds to match your sweatshirts.
2   Design and make some greetings cards to be sold in aid of school funds, for a particular occasion such as Easter, Diwali or other festival.

Computer knitting

EFFICIENCY

In the same way that computerised sewing machines have revolutionised sewing, developments in domestic knitting machines have kept pace. Knitting machines were originally manually operated and in order to change to different stitches, textures and patterns, the operator had to be familiar with many adjustments to dials, levers and discs. More recently, punch card machines allow the design of tuck stitch patterns and Fair Isle (knitting in repeat patterns with two colours per row) through the use of plastic sheets which are punched with holes which the machine can 'read'.

The newest computerised machines simplify the design of knitted fabrics. The operator can design on plastic sheets but holes are not needed. The required design can be drawn free-hand directly on to the special sheet or coloured in on a squared grid. Once the sheet is inserted into the machine and threading completed, the machine will 'read' the design row by row. By pressing lightly on a coded pad, the design may be enlarged, reversed, repeated, elongated and mirror-imaged.

If you do not have access to such a knitting machine in school, it is possible to ask through your teacher, for a local supplier to come into school to demonstrate one. In most large stores there are people who are employed to demonstrate the models that are sold there.

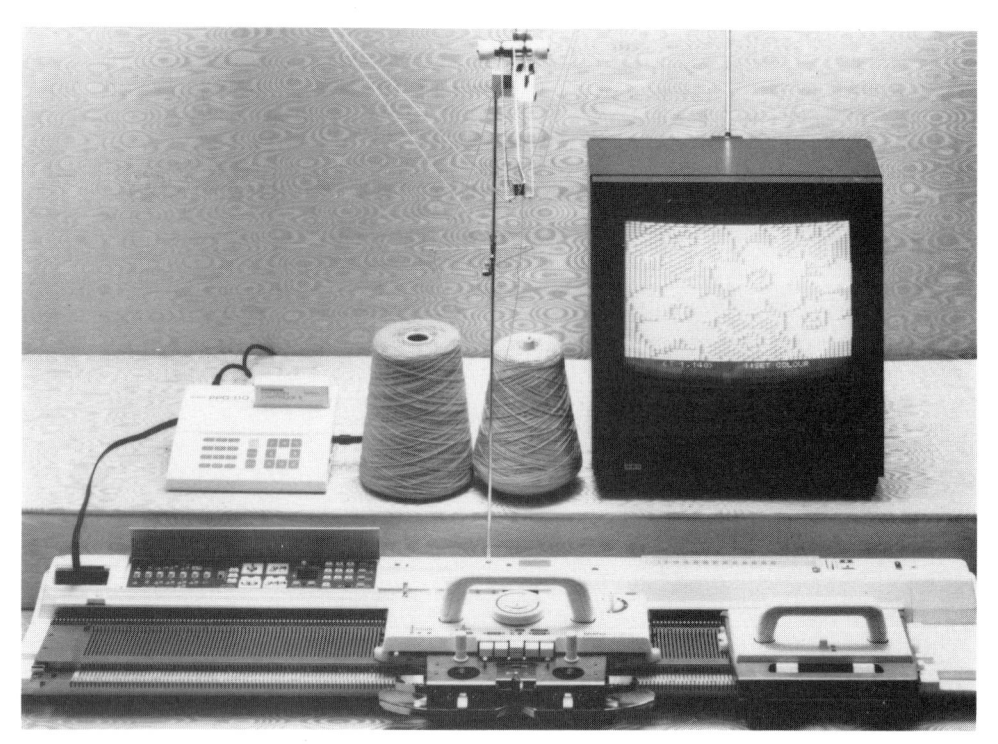

Computerised knitting machine

KEY INVESTIGATION

1. Visit a local store or sewing and knitting centre and watch a demonstration of a computerised knitting machine.
   Or
   Invite a local dealer to come in to demonstrate such a machine to your class.
2. Collect leaflets which promote such machines and give information about them.

▷ **ANALYSIS**

Make a table which illustrates the cost, functions and operation of the machine you have seen demonstrated.

EVALUATION

1 What do you think are the advantages of owning a computerised knitting machine?
2 Why do you think so many knitters give up their machines after a short while? Look in your local paper to find such machines for sale.

INVESTIGATION EXTENSION

If you have access to a knitting machine of any kind, design and knit a piece of fabric for a specific purpose of your own choice. Mount your fabric and sketch a garment which would be suitable to be made up from it. Work out how much the garment would cost to make in the yarn(s) you have chosen.

Index

A

Advertising 126–128
Advertising Standards Authority 128
Appliqué 87

B

Basic blocks 7, 80
Batik 55–58
Blended fibres 18
Block printing 64
Bonded fabrics 35
Brick network 100

C

Chiton 8
Choice 14
Clothing industry 79, 132
Colour 5, 12, 39, 46, 131
Collections 12
Computer 132–136
Computer aided design (CAD) 40, 80–82, 130–131
Computer aided manufacture (CAM) 91, 134
Computer knitting 139
Computer sewing 137–138
Consumer awareness 5, 106, 120
Consumer rights 125
Cutting out 81, 135

D

Design brief 43, 126
Design Council 42
Design loop 43
Design process 10, 38
Designing 10, 38, 80, 82, 126
Dye paint 65
Dye pens, crayons 70
Dyeing process 19, 51

E

Embroidery 73, 74
Envelope plan 13, 14

F

Fancy/novelty yarns 21, 130

Fashion 2, 100, 113
Fashion design 82, 91, 132
Felt 34
Fibres 19, 109
Figure types 4
Form 77
Free machining 96

G

Garment design 79, 80, 82

H

Half drop network 99
Hexagon 101
Home textiles 11

I

Ikat 61
Industrial Revolution 16
Interfacing 35, 81

K

Knitted textiles 25, 31, 32, 33, 139
Knitting 23

L

Labels 16, 109, 110
Laundry 118
Lay planning 80, 133
Line 5, 90–91
Linear patterns 94–95
Looms 26, 27, 28

M

Mail order 122
Methods of payment 124
Mordants 48, 50–51

N

Natural dyes 47, 49, 52
Natural fibres 16, 19
Negative shapes 86
Non-wovens 25, 34

O

Ogee 102

P

Paper patterns 7, 10, 80, 132
Patchwork 104
Pattern 5, 12, 98
Pattern networks 98–102
Performance 113
Ply 20
Poncho 9
Positive shapes 86
Pressing 81, 135

R

Regenerated fibres 18
Resist dyeing 55–63

S

Sari 9
Sale of Goods Act 1979 125
Sewing machine 94–95, 137–138
Shape 77–78, 83–86
Shell 102
Silhouette 4, 91
Smocks 8
Space dyeing 23
Specialist shops 5, 12, 120, 123
Spinning 19–20, 130–131
Square network 99
Stains 119
Starch paste resist 58
Stencil printing 66
Stripes 92–94, 100
Synthetic dyes 54
Synthetic fibres 16, 18

T

Telephone ordering 123, 136
Textile care 117–118
Texture 5, 12, 71–73
Thermoplasticity 18
Tie and dye 58
Toys 83–84
Trade Descriptions Act 1968 128

Transfer dyes 68
Tritik 60

V

Value for money 14

W

Warp 23
Warp knitting 32
Weaves 30
Weaving 25

Weft 23, 26

Y

Yarns 19–23, 130–131